I Didn't Know That!

The Basic Ideas for Successful Relationships

Sharon R. Renfro
9 October 2004

Booklocker.com, Inc.
2003

I Didn't Know That!

The Basic Ideas for Successful Relationships

By

SHARON RENFRO, L.C.S.W.
Licensed Clinical Social Worker

Dedication

To Jean Blackburn who started me on this journey
To Murray Bowen who gave me the gift of theory
to make the journey
And to my daughters, Kathryn and Lillian,
who have taken the journey with me.

Acknowledgements

I would like to acknowledge those persons who read for me, gave me their opinions: a marker of being a Self, and maintained a steady sense of support for this work. You have my gratitude.

PREFACE

I have learned lessons. The lessons presented themselves to me. Through life experiences my lessons represent the same lessons every person encounters as he/she lives life. If we breathe, we learn. Each of us, however, learns something different from the lessons. Most of us just keep repeating what we learned over and over again like a scratched CD that cannot move forward to play the rest of the music. Life becomes a series of disappointments and stagnation. Does this sound like your life?

This patterned response to life traps us in lives we do not want to be living. Like animals caught in traps, we make the same, repetitious, desperate attempts to change things. And, like most animals caught in traps, we eventually give up the desperate fight for change and lie amidst our helplessness to let the inevitable happen.

Few of us want the lives we are living. Most of us are stuck. Hope does not abound in the psychology of our Selves, but no one has offered, to most people, an alternative view to give hope freely as a gift. This book offers that hope, that chance for life to be different.

As I sit writing, reflecting, I sense the deep contentment of being alone. It is the first time in my life that desperation to either be in a relationship or get out of a relationship is not forcing me to behave in ways inconsistent with who I am. It is the first time in my life that I do not see myself as a failure but as a success. I am comfortable with who I am and am not compromising who I am to get into a relationship or to stay in the miserable one I have to keep from being alone. The objective I am working on is to simply continue to be my Self. Could we imagine our lives if that was the primary driving force?

If a relationship comes along that does not require me to fight, run, play dead or pretend to be someone I am not, I may embrace it. But, I want the *choice* of being in the relationship or not. I am lucky. My luck was in meeting Dr. Murray Bowen and studying Bowen Family Systems Theory for a number of years. The theory has offered me a way to understand a series of life mistakes that now I see as amazing opportunities to see an honest reflection of my Self.

This book offers the knowledge for each of us to make that choice for our Selves. Accurate knowledge allows the possibility of wisdom with which we may direct our own lives. The following pages describe a theory of human behavior that gives us the most accurate view of our behaviors to date. The theory, hand in hand with life experience and lessons learned, make this book an effective tool for change. Is change that makes sense the direction we want for our lives?

My current life direction is the direct result of multiple failures. Married and divorced three times permits me to see patterns in what I am doing. No longer can I understand what is happening to me based on who my husband is---I have to see that I am doing something to land my Self in miserable positions. I can see this by using the knowledge I gained in Bowen Family Systems Theory. I can see this, because I made the decisions that I made and can see the desperation that fueled my decisions.

I began four years ago a very careful study of my Self. I used Bowen Family Systems Theory as my guide. Suddenly, before my eyes were patterns that clearly pointed me in a direction I needed to begin a journey toward change. I had assumed that I knew the basic essentials to make a relationship work. What I learned was that I didn't know what I needed to know. A few basic ideas can make a tremendous difference. I had been behaving in very basic ways as I attempted to form and sustain intimate relationships. I am not alone.

Life is lived as it happens. But, life does not have to be predetermined events. It can be a novel set of circumstances with varied solutions available for any situation that arises. Life can be lived from the core of our values and beliefs. Our behaviors can be principled! Can we imagine the benefits of a life true to our values and beliefs---an authentic life? Life lived, based on principles, opens up a whole new realm of possibilities without the constraints of fear.

We are alike. Very few differences separate us. Nature is a part of all of us, and nurture impacted each of us. Some of our experiences are unique, but we all deal with the same emotional process that tells our individual stories. We all can use this book to explore who we really are, to understand the patterns that define our lives, and to meaningfully connect to one another in genuine, intimate ways. All of this can be accomplished by grasping the basic ways we behave in intimate relationships. With this book the choice becomes our very own. It is the things that we do not know that prevent us from having successful, intimate relationships. We do behave in very basic ways in our intimate relationships, and we can know what those are. ***Knowing can give us choice.***

INTRODUCTION

It is how we come to understand what influences our lives that will determine what we finally do. The vast majority of us life our entire lives without this knowledge. That means that we will make mistakes as we go. We make the same mistakes over and over and over again and cannot glean a hint as to what is going wrong. We blame the situation, the circumstance, or someone for the repetitive failures. Most of the time the process that underlies the failures is buried in the heaps of circumstances or people that we blame. The likelihood that we will discover these patterns on our own is minimal. Two major forces influence how we adapt to life: nature and nurture. These forces equip us with adaptive strategies that are supposed to help us to solve our problems. Obviously something goes wrong. Our intimate relationships are less than fulfilling, end before we are off to a good start---often in the divorce court, and provide us little more than isolation and loneliness. This book is meant as an exploration of these issues. It is meant to help us to learn about the two basic forces that have so much to do with the outcome of our lives. It is meant to help us to learn about the impact the teachings of our families have on our lives and our behaviors in intimate relationships. It is meant as a tool to help us to re-learn safety mechanisms that can help us to really find one another in genuinely intimate ways. It is meant as a tool to help us live more "honest" lives without shame or guilt, but with responsibility guided by wisdom. All of this can be achieved. Coming to know who we really are and how we really function is our first step to achieve a contented life.

Life, all life, obeys certain rules of nature. Nature equips animals and plants with a range of behavior from which to select. The behaviors "pre-installed" by nature grant adaptive advantages. One can think of these adaptive tools as mechanisms whose functions are to promote life: to ensure safety. Form and function converge together to secure life for all forms of life. This design is not fail proof, however. These mechanisms work best when we perceive and interpret information accurately. We are prone to error, but these adaptations provide us the best "choice" life forms have for survival. How any organism uses these adaptive mechanisms, at any given point in time, is determined by environmental conditions or by what we have learned is safe or is a threat. As our sense of threat and safety changes, one sees certain behaviors that correspond with each sense. Behavior, therefore, varies with our sense of safety. Variation in behavior can help organisms to survive under varying conditions. In other words, nature equips life, but how we use our equipment depends on how we perceive and interpret what we see. Our perceptions and interpretations are learned. Thus, the interplay between nature and nurture determines our behavior at any given moment in time.

In extreme examples, we can see how nature and nurture works together in response to the environment in ways that sustains life. For example, a fish exists that uses adaptive strategies in ways that result in individual changes so great that one would not recognize the individual as being the same individual. The fish live in a social structure in which one male fish is dominant. The dominant fish grows to proportions much larger than the other fish. His coloration distinguishes him as the dominant fish, as well as other physical features that arm him with the ability to defend him self in ways that other males in the society do not have. His behavior exceeds aggressive tendencies of other males in the group. He is definitely a being with whom the other fish and other species that live in proximity to his group must deal. The interesting fact about this fish is that the fish may not spend its entire life as the dominant fish—dominance hierarchy's change for most species. As the position of dominance changes, dramatic changes in the physical appearance and behavior of this fish occur. A male fish can become dominant, expressing physically and behaviorally his dominance, and then return to being an ordinary fish, while another male takes his place.

The individual male that takes his place, if we looked at him before his succession to dominance, looks like any other male in the group. Strikingly this male fish, that becomes the dominant male, undergoes changes that result in him moving from being one of the group to a fish with whom the rest must reckon. In other words, changes in the environment result in individual changes so extreme that recognition of this fish from previous description would not be possible. Nature allowed the transformation, but the environmental circumstances determined the expression of dominant features and dominant behavior. What can be gathered from this example is that beings change in response to circumstances. Parrotfish can actually change sexes in response to environmental circumstances. Life is filled with examples of amazing transformations based on environmental conditions and circumstances. The same transformations occur in our species.

Lying in our beds we find ourselves lying beside a liar, a conniver, a manipulator. We lie in wait of the next episode in which we will experience the hurt of being betrayed. Our tension is heightened, our awareness of what this other person is up to paramount. We watch, and we devise ways that we can protect our selves. This other person is not to be trusted. Our words are guarded lest we leave our selves vulnerable to being preyed upon by this unscrupulous human being. We search for support from those we consider our friends and build alliances to help us to cope with this relationship. In rare moments, we find some degree of comfort, but being on constant guard leaves us sensing being weary. Our life energy focuses less and less on being productive, creative, and playful creatures, and we become someone we may not recognize our selves. Our behavior, the behavior we deem essential to our protection, leaves us with little self- respect. We know that we are doing things that are "wrong", but we see no alternatives if we are to be safe.

We are not lying in a prison somewhere. We are lying in the bedrooms of our homes beside our partners, a person to whom we have committed the rest of our lives. This is the person with whom we have mated. Our children know us as their parents: the people who will teach them about life and how to have relationships with other people. When we look back at the photos of the day we made these marital commitments, we are stunned, dumbfounded by what has happened. It is as if we are looking at the images of two people we do not even know. We glance in the mirror as we stare at these photos and are over-whelmed by what we see. We recall the days of coming to know this other person, and we wonder what happened, what changed.

15

The changes are not part of our imagination. The extreme changes have happened in both persons. From being two people who genuinely love one another and consider the other person's best interest, we become two people who recognize each other as the enemy. Caught in the recognition that we cannot continue in this relationship much longer, we begin to think of how we may rid our selves of this other person. We experience hurt, remorse, and confusion all of which may lead us, at least for this one day, to try to make things different. When our spouse greets us that day, we may be more open, more available, but in being more open and more available, we have also become more vulnerable.

These respites from the cold war that thrives in our homes are short lived. In only a brief period of time, we will revert back to the warlike behaviors, fully justified for behaving the way we do. Safety, the search for it, is primary and primal. We think about the relief we will experience when this other person is no longer a part of our lives, and we reflect on becoming our old selves again. We yearn just to find safety. Not far from these yearnings, and part of the hope of safety, we begin to fantasize about a different relationship. The tendency is to see the individual as the problem, and when we see the individual as the problem, an automatic solution is replacement of this problematic person with another person who does not have the critical flaws of this individual who shares our bed.

If we knew about the fish described above, it still might be impossible for us to see how much like this creature we are. We, like all forms of life, come equipped with protective mechanisms—adaptive strategies. Once we sense a need to protect ourselves, to secure our safety, we cannot stop our automatic, emotional responses and reason our way through toward a more sensible solution. It is as if automatic pilot takes over our lives. We cannot consider the other person's situation or explanations for his/her behavior. Instinct for safety pushes us forward with our feelings guiding our way through an emotional abyss. Our environments cue us as to when to use these adaptive mechanisms. Most of this operates without our awareness. We are caught in nature's response to threat, and we do not have a clue that this is the case.

We are astute and clever creatures who have the most highly evolved brain on planet earth. In times when we are focused solely on our own safety, we do not use that part of our brain that distinguishes us from other creatures. Our elevation from our relatives gives us the idea that we know what we are doing. If we are superior creatures, surely we know how to have a relationship. As infants our families began to teach us when to be on guard, when we needed protection, and taught us the "appropriate" behaviors to protect our selves. This should be the logical way: the process should make sense. So, as adults, we assume that we know what we are doing in our relationships with one another. We have learned, however, from our families who may or may not be able to distinguish when protective adaptations are advised and when they are not.

If we asked couples to describe what happens between them, we are given explanations. An intriguing fact is that each person has a disparate view from the other person. Each sees him or her self as reporting the truth. From the vantage point of knowing that we "know" exactly what is happening and acceptance that the other person is caught in denial or manipulation, we do not explore other explanations. We behave automatically based on what we know. We fail to think. We behave without asking if our understanding is accurate, how what we are doing influences the other person, or how the other person is experiencing the situation. Without research, reason, and reflection, our intentions can be construed as based on inaccurate assumptions, self-centered, and disrespectful. We do not mean to operate from error, self-centeredness, nor disrespect. It is simply that we do not even recognize that we are behaving this way. We live based on erroneous perceptions and interpretations and do not even know it. Early in life we learn to perceive and interpret, and it that early learning that accompanies us through our lives with relatively little questioning.

Through modern day psychology, we learn that it is pathologies beyond our control that drives us to behave as we do. From seeing our selves as pathological, we have little to no hope of being different. Medications prescribed help to alter some things, but medications must be managed carefully to guarantee even minimal effectiveness. Psychotherapy helps us to address some issues, but psychotherapy has major limitations for effecting real change, in addition to be almost inaccessible to a great number of people. No matter what course we elect to deal with these mental problems, once we begin to sense threat, our behavior becomes pretty much automatic. The reaction of others with whom we relate is predictable. We conclude, therefore, that change is impossible. Our relationships seem to us not viable. If we were able to see that we are simply caught in an instinctual, automatic reaction to being threatened, and if we were able to see that our families have influenced our perceptions and interpretations, then we could find more effective solutions to our relationship problems.

In the 1950s, some researchers in human behavior began to gather clues that alternative explanations to our behaviors were likely to be correct. The information has been slow to reach the average person to make differences in how we understand our selves. As we learn more about other creatures and continue to seek understanding of our selves, we see more and more of these alternative explanations emerging. One of the most important of these researchers, Dr. Murray Bowen, developed a theory to help us to gain a more reliable understanding of our selves. The theory is called Bowen Family Systems Theory. The basic ideas of this theory are that we behave according to the rules of nature tempered by nurture. In other words, we are basically instinctual creatures who are highly influenced by learned perceptions and learned interpretations of those perceptions. Learning is assumed to happen primarily in the context of the family. As couples, we are not reared in the same family, and as a result, our perceptions and interpretations differ widely. The outcome is that we sense threat from our partner not understanding us and acting in a contrary position than what we perceive and interpret to be in our best interests.

Dr. Bowen suggested the most recently evolved structures in the brain could help us to manage our behaviors. By using the forebrain relationships could be calmer and more consistent. Our forebrain, however, is under utilized. With our forebrain, we have the capacity to think. Thinking involves three basic steps. Research is the first step. Research involves gathering objective information: the facts. Reason is the second step. Reason involves understanding how the facts fit together. Reflection is the third step. Reflection involves being able to listen to and hear the emotions, the feelings, and the thoughts of others while maintaining an awareness of our own. Bowen postulated that if we could use this function, we could by-pass the automatic and reactive behavior that promotes relationship dissention. We must find a way to move beyond where we have been in our relationships with each other. This book helps us to find our way. The book begins to help people to learn Bowen Family Systems Theory in simple everyday language that anyone can understand AND use. The ideas presented in the book are basic ideas that make logical sense. Each idea is followed by some clear examples of both ways we currently behave and the potential for us to behave differently. Each chapter has end of chapter ideas that can help readers to apply the knowledge contained in each chapter. The book holds major potential for us to alter the course of our lives. It is an important time for us. We can seize the moment and become better- defined creatures that live in better harmony with each other. We can recognize each other as fellow earthlings who have great potential. The implications reach very far beyond just our own lives. Our children are at stake: their lives are on the line. We teach them, and when we pause to think what it is we teach them, it becomes clear that we are on a course that has limited and dismal outcomes.

When we look across our dining room tables at our mate, we do not have to look at someone we do not even know. We can come to know the conditions, the set of circumstances that are leading to our misunderstandings of each other and the climate that spells threat. Yes, we do have some things in common with fish that transform from being part of the group to being a dominant, fearsome creature. But we do not have to become fearsome creatures in hopes of defending our selves. When we react based on instinctual, primal fears, our hearths are not warmed by the sense of family we create. It is our responsibility to make homes in which each person senses safety and can, from that safe place, define a strong, individual self who recognizes and respects the need for others. We need some simple ideas that work. This book tells us what we did not know.

GLOSSARY OF TERMS

As you read this book, you will be introduced to new terms: a different way of thinking about our selves as we relate to others who are intimate parts of our lives. Using the glossary below will help you to read the book with greater ease and gain understanding of a different way of thinking more quickly. The glossary is not essential, but it is a useful aid. Many people find it helpful to keep this aid beside them as they read.

THEORY: a set of concepts (well developed ideas) that describe and help to explain what happens inside people and between people. These well-developed ideas apply to every self and to every relationship: no exceptions to the "rules". A theory gives us basic ideas upon which we can rely with 100% accuracy.

SYSTEM: a collection of people who have a relationship with each other characterized by each person influencing the others that, in turn, impacts the whole system itself. Each system can be described as to what patterns of behavior dominate the system's responses to relationships based on basic ways human beings behave as they relate.

BOWEN FAMILY SYSTEMS THEORY: a set of concepts defined by Dr. Murray Bowen that describe how family members relate to each other and how those relationships impact the development of an individual self, thus, influencing how we relate intimately with others. BOWEN FAMILY SYSTEMS THEORY defines the basic ideas about how we perceive, experience, and behave in intimate relationships based on learned patterns.

FAMILY SYSTEM: one of our most important and strongest relationship systems formed through marriage and reproduction. This relationship system determines the development of emotional maturity of

20

a self which influences the patterns of behavior that become characteristic to our marriage. It is through the family system that we learn how to perceive, experience, and behave in our relationships with others.

OTHER: a person in our relationship system who influences our own functioning and who's functioning we influence, as the relationship impacts the whole system.

SELF: the internal experience of sensing emotions, feelings, and thoughts for perceiving and interpreting intimate relationship process by using individually defined values, beliefs, and principles to guide our behaviors with others.

EMOTIONS: the instinctual sense of threat perceived by and interpreted through the part of the brain that assess for danger to our selves: our first response for "knowing" if we are safe as individuals in our relationships. Emotions result in one or more of three possible behavioral responses to the environment: to run, to fight, and/or to become immobilized.

R-COMPLEX: the part of the brain that scans our relationships for threat to our selves and produces emotions which results in automatic behavior for protection of our selves when threat is perceived. The only behavioral choices when we use this part of our brain are to run, to fight, and/or to become immobilized.

FEELINGS: the subjective sensations that help us to form and maintain relationships and help us to assess the degree of threat/safety to our selves in our relationships: our second layer of response for "knowing" if we are safe in our relationships. Our feelings assist us to know how serious our senses of threat/safety are and help us to sense the extent of the need to run, to fight, and/or to be immobilized.

LIMBIC SYSTEM: the part of the brain that generates feelings used to help us to know how threatened or how safe we are as individuals in our relationships. This part of our brain helps us to determine to what degree we run, fight, and/or become immobilized.

THOUGHT: a three-step process that is comprised of research, reason, and reflection: the most accurate perception and interpretation of whether or not our selves and others are threatened or safe in our relationships. Thought allows us the possibility of choice in our behaviors.

RESEARCH: the process of gathering objective information about our environment.

REASON: the process of thinking that allows us to identify and understand patterns in relationship systems.

REFLECTION: the process of identifying and understanding the emotions, feelings, and thoughts of another person while maintaining an awareness of our own emotions, feelings, and thoughts. Reflection is the highest order of thought.

NEOCORTEX: the part of our brain that allows us to think: to reason based on facts and reflect based on being part of a relationship system: the only part of the brain that allows us to consider the other person based on facts as part of making relationship decisions. This part of our brain allows us to be able to think, to reason, and to reflect which means we can be a strong self while relating meaningfully to important others in our lives.

VALUE: what a person defines as important to him/her for self and in relationships with others.

BELIEF: what a person defines as accurate perceptions and interpretations about self and intimate relationships.

PRINCIPLE: the guideline one uses to determine behavior based on one's values and beliefs.

CHAPTER ONE

What are we thinking-----or are we?

Truly, a handful of basic ideas can promote a deep level of understanding of our selves, thus allowing us to manage our behaviors in a different way that contributes to openness, permits closeness, and brings us the possibility of the fulfillment of genuine intimacy.

Standing in front of the *Mona Lisa* staring straight into her face, we realize that the woman in this painting is not smiling. In fact, her expression is quite serious. As we begin to turn away, what we see causes us to pause. She smiles. Dumbfounded, we turn straight toward this painting again, and the smile is gone. We shake our heads, rub our eyes, and attempt to clear our vision. Convinced once again that there is not a smile, we turn to leave. Again, the view that we have just formed is shaken. We see the smile from the corner of our eye. What we cannot see straight on, we can see with peripheral vision. Both observations, although greatly different, are accurate.

If we were to accept only one point of view, then we would form certain beliefs. If we take the opposite point of view, our beliefs are the opposite. Were we to hear from one person that they know the *Mona Lisa* does not smile and follow their directions to look straight at the painting without ever getting a peripheral glimpse of the painting, then, we would agree with this person that their view is indeed accurate. We could easily take the side of this person and dismiss the position of person number two who is just as certain the *Mona Lisa* is a painting of a woman who is smiling.

We could believe that the second person is seeing something that is not there: misperceiving what is real. Imagine seeing the smile of the *Mona Lisa* and being unable to convince another person that she is indeed smiling. When we are unable to communicate our point of view to another person, our sense of connection to that person decreases. We sense a degree of threat that they do not "believe" us, that they do not "trust" us. Our experience of a situation may convince us of a point of view, and yet, the other person dismisses us as being "wrong". What can we do? Are we helpless to make a meaningful connection? Is the relationship viable?

It is easy to engage in a headlock with the other person, each believing that they are "right" and the other person is "wrong". When we engage in a headlock, we miss the process that is happening between us. It is the process and not the content of our issues that is stopping us from forming and maintaining stable relationships. With the example of the *Mona Lisa*, each person is "right". How can we set aside the debate and work toward understanding how each person came to hold the point of view they have? Could stopping and gathering the facts, understanding how the facts fit together, and listening to the other point of view help our relationships to be more stable and viable?

What we realize as we think about the different views of the *Mona Lisa* is that we easily accept our perceptions and interpretations of situations as being the only perception and interpretation of a situation. One half of us are divorced. A large percentage of the other half of us live in marriages that do not bring us pleasure or comfort. Something contributes to us ending our marriages, as well as staying in unhappy ones. We have to ask our Selves if we perceive and interpret what happens in our relationships accurately. When each person in a relationship tells us an extremely opposite version of the same situation, we must wonder what is happening. How can this be? How can two people be in the same room and experience the same situation *and* have such vastly different ideas about what happened? Each person sees the same set of facts. Each person watches the same behaviors of everyone in the room. And yet, each person draws very different conclusions. Are we thinking when this situation happens?

We easily accept what we believe we see with little to no question about our accuracy. Unless something puzzles us, we never stop to think about whether or not we are accurate in our view. Nature has given us the ability to act without thinking by immediately assessing a situation and drawing an automatic conclusion. And nature has given us the ability to stop and think before we act. Does *not* thinking make sense?

The answer is Yes but only under certain circumstances. It is to our advantage to act quickly and without hesitation when we are in a dangerous situation. It is to our advantage to stop and think about what is a wise choice in safe and complex situations. Do we have the capacity for both behaviors? If we have the capacity for both, are we thinking when thinking through a situation is to our advantage? Do we know when to instantly react and when to stop and think? If we know when to react and when to think, how do we learn what is best under specific circumstances? We can answer these questions by understanding how our brains developed over time and how our families function as our teachers.

As the brain of human beings developed and changed to its current structures, the changes were additions: not complete makeovers. The old structures remained, and new structures were added on. It is the old structures that give us the ability to act without having to think about the situation in front of us. We do not have to decide what to do. We do not have to choose what to do. We simply react to the situation, as we understand it. The reaction is immediate. The function of such an immediate reaction is to provide us with protection. The old structures prove to be vital when we are in dangerous situations.

The new structures, however, give us the ability to research, reason, and reflect: vital functions in a safe and complex situation. Most of us do not realize that our relationships are complex and safe and require thought for successful negotiation. Both our old brain structures and our new brain structures are helpful to provide us strategies for handling dangerous *and* complex situations. But, when we do not use the "right" strategy for the circumstances, we can find our Selves in trouble. That is where nurture plays a role.

Our families who nurture us teach us to discriminate between what is safe and what poses a threat. Our families teach us when a circumstance is complex and requires us to research, reason, and reflect. So, we have the equipment we need to respond to a wide range of circumstances, and we learn when to use which equipment. Nature and nurture work together to give us the most advantageous strategies for the life circumstances that we face. This sounds like a simple enough formula that would promote our success. If we have the equipment we need and we have the resources to learn how to use our equipment, then we must ask: what is going wrong? The answer is two fold and involves nature and nurture.

NATURE

Nature provided the human being with three layers of perceptual systems with which to perceive and interpret information. The three perceptual systems are the emotional system, the subjective system, and the objective system. The three systems correlate to the three divisions we find in the brain. Each system acts independently and relies on interaction between the systems to perceive and interpret information, but not all three systems function each time we experience a need to perceive and interpret information. This separation and distinction makes sense, because it allows us to not consume massive amounts of time on each and every event we experience. Otherwise, we would be virtually paralyzed to accomplish the basic essentials to keep ourselves alive. To understand what is happening in our relationships with one another, we must have some understanding of what each of these perceptual systems does and how they interface with one another.

The first perceptual system that functions to assess every event we experience is the **EMOTIONAL** system. The emotional system allows us to assess for threat/safety to our Selves. We can react immediately without ever processing the information through either our Subjective or our Objective systems. If our safety is threatened, we react immediately. If we are trying to avoid a car wreck, this immediate reaction to our emotional assessment of threat is our best chance to save our selves from injury. In our relationships with one another, we also constantly assess our safety. If we assume we are safe, we are free to explore, to play, to openly express our Selves, and to make meaningful connections with one another. But, if we assume that our relationship poses a threat to us, we will behave very differently.

If we assume the relationship poses some threat to our safety, we can behave in one of four ways. The four ways are:

RUN: we can attempt to escape the situation. Take for example, the husband who refuses to engage in a conversation with his wife about a sensitive topic. He may listen to her, but he may never respond to her.

He may use many different techniques to avoid ever talking to her about what she wants to discuss with him. He simply avoids the situation altogether.

FIGHT: we can attempt to defend our Selves by fighting and hopefully winning. A wife may become loud and aggressive when she thinks she needs to defend her Self. A husband coming home late from work may dread coming in the front door, because he knows that his wife will be ready for a confrontation.

CAMMOUFLAGE: we can attempt to keep our Selves safe by pretending that the situation that is happening is not really happening. A husband can tell his wife for years that the affair she accuses him of having is not really happening. He can tell her that she has a trust issue on which she needs to work. He can pretend to still be in love with her and play out the part. She can easily slip into the pretend with him and make believe that he is a faithful husband.

PLAY DEAD: we can attempt to keep our Selves safe by playing dead. Acting as if we are safe in a situation in which we are not is a common attempt at protection. A husband can become helpless and unable to function as a way to keep his wife from leaving him when he knows she is engaged in an affair.

As we can see, when we sense a threat, we can respond in a limited number of ways, and none of these strategies would be considered helpful to an intimate relationship. The behaviors are very different than the behaviors we see when we perceive and interpret our relationship to be safe. We can know, beyond a shadow of a doubt that the behaviors are destructive to our relationship, and yet, when threatened engage in these behaviors as if our lives depended upon the protection. Can we see how differently we behave with those we love when we sense being safe with that person versus when we sense that the person is a threat to our well-being? When we think this way, does it make sense that our relationships are in trouble? Do we have strategies available to us to prevent this destructive behavior that occurs when we misperceive whether or not our partner poses a threat?

Yes, the next level of perception gives us additional data to help us to assess the degree of threat or safety we sense. The second perceptual system is the **SUBJECTIVE** System. Our feelings are the result of the Subjective System. While feelings can help us to clarify our degree of threat/safety, feelings can also muddy the waters and make assessments less reliable. For example, if we are walking down a dark, city street and see someone approaching us, we have a very different response if we recognize the person as someone we love versus recognizing the person as a stranger to us. In this situation, our feelings may help to save our lives. If however, we go back into a violent relationship in which we are being physically beaten because we "love" the person who is beating us, then our feelings have muddied the waters. Our feelings may or may not be reliable indicators. Feelings are merely meant to help us with gross refinements of our emotions. They may help us to act more quickly to protect our Selves, or feelings may help us to pause long enough to think through our situation. If feelings are meant as gross indicators of our safety or threat, how come we behave as if we can depend on our feelings as very reliable indicators to tell us what to do?

Feelings may be very strong at any given moment in time, only to dissipate as rapidly as they happened. The strength of a feeling is used to guide us in our decision-making. Strong love can transform into intense anger in a matter of seconds. The intense anger can turn back into strong love just as quickly. And yet, we rely on our feelings to guide us in our relationships with each other. In a dark alley when we need a quick assessment if we are safe or not, feelings can save our lives. We can rely on our feelings in these circumstances to actually perform one of the functions for which they were designed. In more complex relationship situations, however, feelings are unreliable indicators, because they are too strongly tied to our sense of safety or threat. With our feelings tied to our emotions and likely to change rapidly to opposite extremes, does it make sense to rely on feelings to tell us what to do in our most important relationships? If our emotions do not give us reliable strategies in our intimate relationships and our feelings do not offer much more assistance, then does the third perceptual system give us any hope for a more reliable guidance system?

Our **OBJECTIVE** System does give us the tools we need to factually distinguish between threat and safety. Thought provides us tools to regulate our emotions and our feelings. This does not mean that we ignore or suppress our emotions and feelings: it simply means that we manage our behavior by over-riding our emotions and feelings. We override our emotions and feelings by using thought. It is only when we can reliably distinguish between real threat and real safety that we can afford to experience deep emotion or deep feelings without having endangering our Selves. If this is the case, then what promotes our use of our emotions and our feelings without engaging in thought?

The problem is that in order to access the tools of thought, we must recognize a need to use them. In other words, we need to realize that we do not know what to do and that we do not understand what is happening. Some puzzle, such as the *Mona Lisa* smiling and not smiling, must happen for us to engage in the process of thought. When we experience being dumbfounded, it is only then that we then turn to thought.

Thought is actually a three-step process. The first step is to Research. The second step is to Reason. The third step is to Reflect.

RESEARCH: we use our ability to research when we collect information or facts about a situation. It is simply the gathering of the facts: who, what, when, where and how.

REASON: we use our ability to reason when we recognize and understand how the information or facts fit together. In other words, it is the "ah ha" when the puzzle pieces fit together.

REFLECTION: we use our ability to reflect when we recognize, understand, and take into consideration the other person's emotions, feelings and thoughts while also being able to do the same for our Selves.

Objectivity is available to everyone, but we must be taught to use it. We must know that we need to think. Nature has pre-installed all of these functions, but it is the first two functions that are truly vital to our survival. When we are in an intimate relationship, our survival is not at stake. The problem is that we react as if it is. We expend a great deal of life energy in relationships trying to defend our Selves. The remarkable thing is that we are really threatened. At other times we spend immense amounts of life energy in a relationship behaving as if we are safe when we are actually not safe at all. Knowing the difference is a function of our third perceptual system and involves the process of thought. So, how does it happen that we recognize the need to think?

HOW PERCEPTUAL SYSTEMS WORK TOGETHER

In order to help us understand how the three perceptual systems work together, we can take a look at how traffic engineers put up traffic lights and promote the safety of drivers. Living in a city gives us the opportunity to observe what happens when a traffic light is installed in an intersection. Of course, when we travel a route routinely, we learn what we need to do without constantly being on guard. Think for a minute about the difference in our driving habits when we are driving in a strange city versus making the drive home each night after work. Our degree of being alert and on guard diminishes when we are doing the routine. We have learned the route, and we do not need to use very much life energy to make the trip every day.

Traffic engineers may have noticed a pattern of accidents at a particular intersection. From these patterns, they design a study to collect the facts about what happens as we travel through the intersection. Once the facts are collected, the traffic engineers begin to study the information to establish patterns and understand how the patterns may need to change to aid the flow of traffic and increase the likelihood of safety. These ideas are then studied from various angles, reflecting on how other variables will also influence the design. Things such as traffic flow at different times during the day, businesses that may be more frequently used at different times of day, turns that disrupt the flow of traffic are taken into account. These facts influence what happens in the intersection we travel, and if traffic engineers simply install a traffic light without looking at the many variables that influence it, they may install a traffic light and make an intersection more dangerous than it was. Looking at an intersection without regard to other variables can result in making matters far worse than they had been before. We may think that the installation of a traffic light is a simple matter when, indeed it is not.

After the traffic engineers have completed their studies, they make recommendations. If the public officials decide to install a traffic light, certain steps are followed and for very good reasons. We probably do not understand the reasoning for all these steps, but our safety is at stake based on the procedures followed. On our way to work, we may notice the trucks putting the traffic light up, and be surprised on our way home from work that the lights are not working. Traffic engineers do not put a light up and turn it on to regulate traffic all in the same day.

What happens is that the light is placed on flashing. The street that had the right of way is placed on flashing yellow. We are told, in essence, continue to pass through this intersection today but be aware that you need to look at this light to tell you what to do. The street that had to stop before proceeding forward is placed on flashing red. We are told, in essence, continue stopping at this intersection and look for traffic. When the way is clear, proceed through the intersection, but be aware that you need to look at this light to tell you what to do. As we approach our intersection, the flashing light tells us that we must do something different than has been done before. In other words, we are doing the exact same thing as we were the day before, but now we are being alerted to the fact that something is going to change.

We sense that our safety is at issue, we may become slightly anxious, but we will definitely begin to think as we approach this intersection. We will research by gathering information about what is expected of us to stay safe. We may slow down slightly or begin to think about which lane we need to be in if a turn arrow is also involved. The point is that we will not just proceed through the intersection without thinking about it. As we gather information, we being to reason about what patterns may be established by the new traffic light. We reason by drawing conclusions about what new traffic pattern will be established. And finally, we reflect about how what we will do in the future will fit with what the other drivers will be doing. If there is a turn arrow and we are going straight, we may want to use the right lane to continue driving without having to stop. We can anticipate that we will have to wait longer to turn than we used to have to wait. We may find that we need to be in the far turn lane, so as to be in the correct lane when we reach our destination. Many things may change, and we will adapt if we have thought through these steps.

This process changes what we knew in the past to what we need to know to be safe in the future. This process takes about three weeks of repeating over and over thinking through the situation as we approach it. At that time, the stop signs can be removed, and the lights can begin to function to regulate the traffic flow. We have learned that we need to do something different, and we have learned what we need to do to be safe. Relationships are the same way.

We need some kind of flashing light to alert us that we need to think about what is happening to us and come up with some kind of a plan based on facts that will take into consideration other people. The flashing light should be that we are divorcing in record-breaking numbers and that we are living in unhappy marriages. We eat anti-depressants and anti-anxiety medications without concern about what is really the problem. We try to make the symptoms go away that are the very flashing lights we need to see to stop and think. If the symptoms stop, then we do not need to think about what is "wrong". Of course, that is like traffic engineers just putting up a traffic light with disregard for other variables that influence the safety of people at the intersection. A great deal of patterns can be covered up by years of events.

What keeps us from pausing and thinking in the face of these facts is that we believe we have explanations that are correct. In order to assure our safety, we must engage in the three steps of thinking and not settle for a divorce to get rid of the person we married who is causing the problem. We must go beyond deciding to make the best of the situation that we got our Selves into. We must risk learning about who we are even though the process takes time. Traffic engineers do what is required to ensure the safety of the public. Can we decide to really research, reason, and reflect to make sure we are as safe in our personal relationships?

What we are missing in our lives is the traffic light: we have no way to regulate our relationships except for what we have learned from our families as their strategies to relate. We need a way of knowing what information to gather, a way to understand how the pieces of the puzzle fit (just like having a box to the puzzle so we "get" the idea of what the puzzle pieces make), and a way to reflect on all the people involved to ensure that no one is harmed, and everyone has the potential of sensing being safe. So, what can we do to unlearn and relearn more effective strategies that will keep us safe in our relationship?

NURTURE

Families teach us to distinguish between when we are safe and when we are threatened. The lessons are completely learned by at least age six, so most of these lessons take place prior to having memories of the lessons. When we learn lessons from our parents, we are learning the lessons that they learned from their parents. The process is, therefore, multi-generational. Knowing that multiple generations impact our current functioning can be comforting, not only for us but also for our parents. In other words, no one person is to blame. Our current life situation is the accumulation of multiple lives trying to find their way through the maze of relationship functioning without benefit of an accurate way to think. That means that no one person has made a life mistake all on his/her own. It also means that no one person has made correct life decisions all on his/her own. Experiences teach life lessons, but we can draw the wrong conclusions. Our only way to change is to be able to research, reason, and reflect, but if our parents have not taught us how to do this, then we must learn to do it on our own.

It is difficult to access information about the lessons and how they were taught. Finding out what we were taught is not impossible. It is possible to gather information about our families that can give us enough solid evidence to reconstruct what we learned. One window into what we have learned from our parents comes from detailing our values, beliefs, and principles.

It is our values, beliefs, and principles that give us our definition of our Selves as individual human beings. Our values, beliefs, and principles determine whether or not we perceive and interpret relationship events as safe or threatening to us. Knowing our values, beliefs and principles is a critical part of making a difference in our relationships. But what are values, beliefs, and principles, and how can these make differences in our relationships?

A VALUE is what we accept as important to our well-being. A BELIEF is what we understand to be factual and accurate. A PRINCIPLE is the guideline we use to determine our behavior and is derived from our values and our beliefs. These seem "right" to us, so even if our relationships are not working out the way we would like for them to, we continue to use our values, beliefs, and principles to tell us what to do in our relationships. What seems natural to us is what we do. It is like driving home the same way every evening: we do not have to think. We simply drive. In our relationships, we simply behave based on what we have been taught to do. If something is going wrong in our relationships, we come up with an explanation as to "why" based on what we have been taught. It is amazing that so many things can go wrong in a relationship, and we do not stop to question if we are accurate. An example may help.

If we take two people, Rebecca and Josh, who are beginning a relationship, we can begin to see how values, beliefs, and principles influence relationship decisions. The relationship is about four months old, and an old girlfriend has come on the scene. Rebecca is immediately concerned about the old girlfriend. Although she thinks that Josh is honest with her, she has observed him tell his parents lies when he does not want to them to know something he has done. In other words, she senses being safe most of the time but questions if Josh would lie to her the way he does to other people. Rebecca values telling others what she really thinks in important relationships. She believes that the best way to work through any issues and reach some kind of resolution is to talk. So, she talks to Josh about her concerns about his old girlfriend.

Josh values not having any conflict. He senses being safe when conflict is non-existent. He believes that if conflict erupts in a relationship, it can destroy the relationship. He really likes Rebecca and wants the relationship to work out. When she brings up her concerns about the old girlfriend, Josh becomes really scared. He does not want to talk about the issue, because he is scared that they will argue. He reassures her that the old girlfriend is not important. Since Josh cannot talk to Rebecca about the issue, because he is afraid he will ruin their relationship, he talks to his old girlfriend about it. We all know what happens next: Rebecca finds out that Josh has seen his old girlfriend again.

Rebecca senses being safe when she and someone important to her talk about issues that come up between them. She does not sense being safe with Josh not having talked to her. If we talked to Rebecca and Josh, we might find that we have the same experience if we had talked to the two people who saw the *Mona Lisa* from very different points of view. Each has good points. But until each person understands their own values, beliefs, and principles and the values, beliefs, and principles of the other person, the relationship will continue to present the same patterned problems.

When we look at what Rebecca's parents taught her, we find that they had a great deal of conflict. The marriage eventually ended in divorce. Rebecca had believed that if her parents could have talked through their problems, they would have been able to save their marriage. She valued talking. That was her solution to fix a problem. When we look at Josh's family, we find that his parents have never engaged in any conversation that could result in conflict. Josh had repeatedly been told not to bring up subjects that could be considered sensitive to the other person, but then people talked about their concerns about the other person with someone else. Josh knew, beyond a shadow of a doubt, that talking about things could lead to something very dangerous in a relationship. He also needed someone to talk to who presented a minimal risk for conflict to develop. His ex-girlfriend was that person, although most people would say that would not be the wise choice in this situation.

The point is that nature and nurture converge in our relationships. It is important to know about how these two forces interface. This book can be our *Mona Lisa*. It can be our flashing light to help us to see that we must begin to do something different in our relationships with one another. As each chapter describes a basic way we behave in our relationships with each other, the interface between nature and nurture helps us to understand what is happening in our relationships. From understanding we can formulate solutions that can allow us to have rich and meaningful relationships with one another. We can stand in front of our lives and not have to deny what we see or ask the other person to discount their point of view. We can begin to understand that we simply come from different vantage points, both of which can contribute to the overall well-being of our relationship. This means we must employ thought.

We must begin to distinguish our values, beliefs, and principles from those of our families. The steps toward making a difference in our relationships can be taken one at a time without the painful experience we traditionally think of when we think of an "over-haul". We are from planet earth. We have more in common with each other than we have differences. *Truly, a handful of basic ideas can promote a deep level of understanding of our selves, thus allowing us to manage our behaviors in a different way that contributes to openness, permits closeness, and brings us the possibility of the fulfillment of genuine intimacy. After all, is that not what all of us really wants?*

END OF CHAPTER WORK

1. LIST RELATIONSHIPS IN WHICH YOU EXPERIENCE SENSING SAFETY.

2. WHAT ABOUT THESE RELATIONSHIPS PROMOTE A SENSE OF SAFETY FOR YOU?

3. THINK ABOUT YOUR MOST RECENT RELATIONSHIPS: WHEN DID YOU BEGIN SENSING NOT BEING SAFE?

4. WHAT ABOUT THIS RELATIONSHIP DOES NOT PROMOTE A SENSE OF SAFETY IN YOU?

5. AS YOU REVIEW CHAPTER ONE, WHAT IDEAS WERE MOST IMPORTANT TO YOU? WHAT DO YOU THINK MAKES THESE IDEAS IMPORTANT?

CHAPTER TWO

What Is a Basic Fact?

>*When we can step back from the intensity of our relationships, we have a greater possibility of being objective about what happens in our relationships. Objectivity means that we can think---we can describe the facts, know how the facts fit together, and behave in a way that respects our Selves as well as the person who is most important to us.*

From the dark expanse of space far above our home planet, a telescope attached to a satellite captures a view of the cosmos. In this sea of darkness, our illuminated planet seems small and more inconsequential than the sense we have from our daily lives. We sense a high degree of importance as we go about our daily lives: a sense that seems not quite so critical as we look down on our planet from space. Individual importance gives way to an increased awareness that we share this planet with thousands of life forms. We watch weather patterns moving from one continent to the next impacting what happens to individual lives and suddenly see that even with thousands of miles of distance we are connected.

Seeing a more global picture helps us to see a connectedness to one another that we cannot sense on a day in day out basis. We become more aware that we are only a small part of a whole, bigger picture. From this view of the whole, our perceptions of all the individual parts change. The distinction between individuals blurs as the view of a planet in which patterns impact the well-being of the parts becomes clearer and clearer. Stepping back releases us from a narrow point of view, and what we can see and how we can understand what we see changes dramatically. Without a telescope in space, we are bound to views that offer limited accuracy in understanding our world.

Moving away from our every day existence, we discover a different perspective that was not possible from the confines of earth.

Even from a telescope at a planetarium, we cannot see the intricacy of our connections to each other. Looking back from space, we find facts about our selves that bind us together and alter the perception of "individuality". It is then that our information about our planet takes a divergent view that will lead to us altering many ideas generated from prior knowledge. *New observations allow us to formulate new knowledge.* With new knowledge, we can know more about our planet, our relationship to one another, and from that vantage point make informed, responsible decisions. With new knowledge, we have new choice about our response to each other and to our planet. Risking knowing more means that we can potentially alter our understanding, hopefully with the outcome being responsible action.

Our planet, in contrast to the cold vastness of space, appears warm and inviting----a place to call home. And yet, we also capture a view of how fragile our planet truly is. Earth may teem with life, but resources must sustain life. We can become more factual about what threats we really face, we can with these facts understand our connections, and finally we can be more responsible in how we behave in relation to our universe. New knowledge has led us to major changes in our course of action.

Distance can be very clarifying. Clarification can be very sobering. What we cannot know from being too close, we can learn from stepping back to a broader view. Does objectivity sound like it is missing from our lives? Can we achieve this level of functioning?

In the 1950s, a handful of professionals began to step back from studying the individual to studying families for clues about human behavior. They essentially strapped a telescope onto their backs and observed the human being as a part of a larger system. As they moved away from the human being to a larger perspective, they began to collect facts not seen before. The most important person in this new research was Dr. Murray Bowen. In order to learn how to be more objective, it is important to know how Dr. Bowen was able to describe what we do in relationships with each other. The process he followed is the exact same process that we can use to help us.

A few professionals who had studied Freudian Theory began to ask questions related to the limits of Freudian Theory. The limitations that resulted in these questions being asked had to do with not being able to help people who were experiencing problems by using Freudian Theory. When we have evidence that something is not working, an important step to discovery of more accurate information is to question the basis of the thinking that is currently accepted as being accurate. Dr. Bowen observed the limitations of Freudian Theory during World War II when he was stationed in England. In England, he had questions about how come Freudian Theory could not help service men who were experiencing severe symptoms related to their battle experiences. The experience led Dr. Bowen to alter his life course from surgery to psychiatry.

Upon returning to The United States, he enrolled at Menninger's Clinic, the premier training facility in the states to learn Freudian Theory. His interest was research. His goal was to study Freudian Theory and advance the helpfulness it could provide to treat mental and nervous disorders. As he posed research questions and began to collect information, he could not make the information gathered "fit" into Freudian Theory. He eventually moved his research to The National Institute of Mental Health in Bethesda, Maryland, where he expanded his research. The expansion of the research allowed him to collect more facts. At NIMH, he was able to hospitalize entire families for observation. Again, he stepped further away from a focus on the individual to focus on the larger system.

With new facts, he began to try to understand how these facts fit together to result in patterned behavior. The next step was to understand how the behavior of each person impacted all others in the system. In other words, Dr. Bowen researched, reasoned, and reflected. It is the same process that we can use to understand this theory and alter the course of our relationships. As he did so, he formulated a new theory: Bowen Family Systems Theory.

The theory was based on the idea that nature and nurture interact resulting in human behavior. It is built upon the idea that adaptations can be helpful if adaptations are used in the appropriate situations. The ideas are simple ones. The ideas give us many points of intervention from which we may alter our life courses. Can we imagine how we could influence our relationships with each other if we had a reliable theory that was derived from common sense?

By using Bowen Family Systems Theory, we can step back from the intensity of our own lives and begin to collect the facts about what is happening. With the theory, we can begin to understand how all the facts fit together and result in our behaviors. Then, we can take into account everyone in the relationship and make wiser decisions based on solid knowledge.

This book takes us step by step through the first three basic ideas of Bowen Family Systems Theory. It does so using everyday language and examples that can help us to change our relationships. We can see how nature and nurture impact our behaviors and can begin to define our Selves in the context of our relationships with others based on carefully defined values, beliefs, and principles. Objectivity is possible. Our relationships can be understood: we do not have to live in some kind of mystery that isolates us and keeps us from being meaningfully connected to each other.

Dr. Bowen gave the world a gift. He strapped a telescope to a family and took a long-term view of human history. From both advantage points, he has given us some basic facts about how we behave in intimate relationships. This information gives us the freedom to explore, to become close to one another without losing a sense of our own individual selves, to calm the intense and extreme anxieties that accompany us in our daily lives, to separate out the real threats from the ones we imagine, to direct our own lives from knowledge, and thus, from wisdom, to help our children to learn far different ways to interact that does not destroy relationships. We have hope. That hope lies in our commonality, an essential ingredient for any fact to be basic. We have the strategies that we need.

Bowen Family Systems Theory offers us a way to research, reason, and reflect to make these strategies accessible to us. From the vast expanse of space, we have a new view. We can see what we have not seen before. We can know and find safety in that knowledge. We can pull back, find the patterns, know our connections, and set forth on the journey of life filled with remarkable life experiences. Each of us has our own beacon of light with which we can find our own way. It is with these facts that the mysteries of our intimate lives fade away. What emerges is hard evidence---solid ground on which we can stand as we move forward through the challenges any one life time faces. We are from planet earth, and there are basic ways that we do behave. *Distance can be very clarifying. Clarification can be very sobering. What we cannot know from being too close, we can learn from stepping back to a broader view.*

END OF CHAPTER WORK

1. Think of two situations in which you believed you knew what was happening in a relationship only to find out later that you did not know.

2. List the differences between how you first handled the situation and what you did after you found out you were in error.

3. What helped you most to know that your own conclusions were inaccurate?

4. Review Chapter Two and think about what ideas are most important to you. What makes these ideas helpful to you? How do you think you can use these ideas to make a difference in your intimate relationships?

CHAPTER THREE

Basic Way We Behave #1
People Are Aware of Each Other and Respond to One Another

>*From our understanding we decide how to function. Our perceptions and interpretations affect our lives daily and determine what major life decisions we make. We move toward what we believe is safe and away from what we sense as threatening.*

Imagine a time long before science; our ancestors huddle together around a fire trying to stay warm on the African plains as darkness surrounds them. Stars begin to dot the sky, and the moon rises over the horizon illuminating the night. The light of the moon gives a sense of security that the night will bring no surprises. As our ancestors talk and plan the next day, something unusual begins to occur. In the middle of the night sky, the moon begins to gradually disappear and is eventually gone altogether. The world becomes darker: a scarier place. Our ancestor's watch, probably with a great deal of fear, as a phenomena happens which cannot be understood. They lacked the knowledge, but they probably did not lack explanations.

The explanations likely did not come close to approximating the facts, but the explanation served a purpose. Myths become truths in attempts to quell the anxiety of experiencing the unknown. Having some kind of explanation for an occurrence helps us to also have a solution or a way to correct what we experience. Believing that we understand what is happening gives us some sense of being able to do something about our situations. Confusion oftentimes leads to despair. Whether or not our explanations are accurate seems far less important than believing that we know. If we have a problem with our spouse, believing that their currently diagnosed psychiatric disorder is causing our spouse to behave the way they are gives us a sense of relief. If we know what is wrong, then we stand some chance of fixing it. Our ancestors came up with many explanations that we know today as nonsense. To believe that some god is displeased or that the disappearance of the moon is an omen, a sign, offers some kind of assurance that being left in a quandary of being uncertain cannot offer.

In explanations, one searches for understanding that can help one to know one's universe is safe and predictable: we can do something to ensure our safety. We invoke simplistic cause and effect explanations of good and evil. We perform rituals for protection to ward off the evils that surround us, hoping to secure our safety. We remain hyper-alert for such evils, and yet our hyper-alert state can seem like so much childish folly when we learn that our explanations are far removed from "truth". Our explanations are important to us. We do not shed them easily, even as we collect information, the facts that tell us we are dead wrong.

Being dead wrong eventually can give way to seeking the truth. The "truth" remains the truth until enough evidence accumulates to correct "knowledge", although that can be a very long time. In the interim period, we pay prices for hanging onto myths. Knowledge changes as facts change. Using new knowledge for our well-being depends on how quickly we can assimilate the new information in our understanding of our world. How quickly we can do that depends on how safe we sense in letting go of old beliefs. As long as we are convinced that we are right, we will seek no further for the truth. As long as we sense safety by hanging onto our belief systems, we will not move toward change. We must be able to live with a degree of uncertainty, the product of not knowing, to not settle for myths. Time, if paired with the seeking of knowledge, changes our view, alters our understanding. >*From our understanding, we decide how to function. Our perception and our interpretation of facts impact our lives daily and determine what major life decisions we make.* Can we use new knowledge to help us with our personal relationships? Do we believe in myths that are standing in the way of relationship happiness?

Deep in the recess of our brains we carry with us a black and white view of life. It is a rulebook that accompanies us through life with no demands to pause and think. At some level this black and white view moves us more smoothly through our day. At another level, it results in long-term complications that can cost us dearly in how our black and white interpretation of the world impacts our relationships. The primary myth we use in our intimate relationships is that we are to become one when we love someone and commit to them. The myth promotes a sense of isolation, loneliness, disappointment, hurt, and a multitude of other negative feelings. In other words, when any event presents itself in which our partner has not acted in the best interest of THE UNIT, we sense a degree of threat. The interesting dilemma is that when we sacrifice what is in our own best interest in favor of the relationship, we then can sense threat to our SELVES. This poses a major problem for relationship stability. Does it not make sense that if we understand this process, we can lessen the challenge for the relationship?

If a person can see what has been thought of as a relationship problem simply as a natural process, then the degree of threat experienced diminishes. With a decreased sense of threat, we are more likely to engage in research, reason, and reflection. The likelihood of finding a solution to the situation then increases. A solution that is the result of research, reason, and reflection will be one that enhances the well-being of both partners as well as the relationship itself. Does this sound like the way we would like our relationships to work? For us to be able to do that, we must understand the impact of nature and nurture on the development of our SELF.

NATURE

Nature is fundamental to all life. Nature is our instincts and inherent tendencies that direct our behaviors. Certain instinctual tendencies are shared by all life forms. The first is the recognition that self is distinct from other organisms. This recognition of Self that all life forms share is very rudimentary and instinctual. For example, all life recognizes a need for nutrition on an individual level. The coinciding behavior is automatic and very basic. For example, all life engages in behavior to obtain needed nutrients. These rudimentary responses to the environment help to protect life forms from dying. Although these strategies are not always successful, the automatic behaviors represent the best opportunity for survival. Survival is a common instinctual urge of all organisms, including us. All organisms when aware of a threat behave in ways to attempt to protect themselves. In order to activate the protective behaviors, an organism must recognize a threat as a threat. Failure to recognize a threat may lead to demise of the organism. Knowing a threat from something that is safe does require learning.

The most rudimentary behaviors to protect our Selves involve our basic needs. Our awareness of our Selves as individuals in regard to our basic needs is the first level of awareness of Self. The behaviors of seeking, obtaining and processing the resources to meet our needs are all instinctual. It is only later in our lives that we gain an awareness of our Selves as distinct entities that can function independent of others. We become more aware of others as we gain more awareness of Self. The skills needed to negotiate these more complex relationship systems are something that we learn as we gain this awareness. To whatever degree we perceive of our Selves as separate and distinct entities and are able to function as independent, distinct Selves will be the same degree of skill level we have mastered. We accomplish these tasks in our development through the perceptual systems given to us by Nature. We learn how to use these perceptual systems through Nurture.

As we physically mature, thus gaining the ability to function more independently, we also mature in how we use our perceptual systems. As infants, we must take in nutrients, we must regulate the level of nutrients and waste in our bodies, we must restore our Selves and we must behave in ways that promote our physical safety. Relationships provide us the possibility of safety. The simpler the organism, the less reliant on learning the organism is for its protection. By the time we move on up the phylogenetic scale to the top rung, we find an organism that requires the longest time to reach maturation and independent functioning. That means that the interplay between Nature and Nurture is critical to our success in achieving maturation.

EMOTIONS

The emotional system monitors our environment for safety or threat. It is always working. It is our first line of response to our environment. Until we have assessed our environment for safety or threat, we are not free to explore our world on any other level. This ensures our safety and is a throw back from our days on the plains of Africa when our physical well-being was threatened on a very regular basis. Our brains still come equipped with this perceptual system, and in certain circumstances it is an essential function. Our assessments become much more complex as we age and become less dependent on another human being for our safety. Our awareness of our Selves, our awareness of others, and our skills to relate to others in ways that promotes our safety as an individual human being develop simultaneously.

As an infant, we move from a very rudimentary awareness of our needs. We have very rudimentary responses to these needs. Our responses are suppose to elicit in others care giving behaviors that promote surviving and thriving. Whether or not our needs are met depends on the ability of our caregivers to perceive and interpret correctly our needs. If our caregivers are unable to respond with the appropriate behaviors, then we may fail to survive or fail to thrive. This presents us with major implications for our futures. Parents function on many different levels of awareness of Self, and the degree of awareness and skills achieved to encourage mature, independent functioning they have achieved will be a gauge of their success in helping off-spring to achieve maturation. Many circumstances can influence this process and impact the degree of success any parents have to the end point of maturation. If parents are successful in providing a child with a sense of safety, then the child progresses in his/her development.

When we look at the ability of a small child to function totally on his/her own, the odds are against a child to function independently and survive and thrive. However, under optimal conditions a young child may be able to survive without caretakers to ensure their safety. We still see a being incapable of reliably distinguishing between real threat and safety. Many parents must proceed through a series of reassurances at bedtime that a child's room is safe from harm. The child cannot manage these fears with research, reason, and reflection independent of their parents. Parents must help their child to gather the facts about the monster under the bed, reason for the child about how these facts go together to make the situation safe, and then reflect on how the relationship system can help the child to feel safe. Reassurance paired with the perceptual system of thought can help a child to become calm and fall asleep. As small children, we cannot research, reason, or reflect. We are dependent on others for this process. Depending on someone else is the only way for us to deal with our emotions until we can research, reason, or reflect.

To gain some insight into what it is like to not be able to research, reason, and reflect, we can think about our dreams. The function of rest is to restore us and to give our brains time to file away the information of the day, discarding what is not necessary and cataloging what we need to retain. We prepare for the following day when massive amounts of information will need to be processed. Without a clear desk, so to speak, processing the next day's information becomes impossible. We rely on research, reason, and reflection to prevent us from living our lives as if we were in a dream state. Rest is essential to us, and without it we can develop symptoms that can debilitate our functioning. What we find as we dream is that we abandon all research, reason, and reflection. Our minds are filled with emotions, and we create situations in which we are safe or threatened.

We can experience highly pleasurable dreams in which our minds create situations in which we are safe. These dreams are usually filled with feelings that we regard as positive. We also can experience highly frightening dreams in which our minds create situations in which we are not safe and are unable to take protective measures. These dreams are usually filled with feelings that we regard as negative. It is only when we wake that we can use our research, reasoning, and researching abilities to help us resolve the dream we just had. Without thought, we are left with our emotions and our feelings and no way to logically deal with them. We become totally reactive creatures. Does this sound like what we think of as teenagers? Does this sound like the life we are leading as adults: a life that does not make sense but we do not know our way out of the situation?

Until late in our teens, we are unable to research, reason, AND reflect. We have gained some skills to research and reason, but we have not learned the skills we need to reflect. We can appear as if we are uncaring and illogical. We are still in the stages of learning. If at this time, our parents begin to sense our pulling away from them as a threat to the relationship that had been close with them, their reactions can interfere with our learning to reflect. Practice is required to gain the skills necessary to become mature.

We learned that it takes quite a bit of practice to learn traffic rules when a new traffic light is installed. More practice is needed for a complex relationship system. To not practice means that we are restricting the development of Self, and we will not reach optimal maturation. Teens sense this type of restriction as a threat. When threatened, we all have limited behaviors from which to select. The typical response we have as teens to our parents attempts to restrict our learning is to turn to other people like our Selves. At the very time we could benefit from instruction from people who are mature, we turn to other teens that do not have the skills of reflection either. The outcome is exactly what we would assume it to be.

Things can go "wrong" in each of these stages of development. When things go "wrong", we can end up not moving forward in our emotional maturation. Instead of becoming a thoughtful human being who can research, reason, and reflect, we become stuck in our emotions. We are stuck in our emotional responses with no alternatives to behave differently.

Our behaviors are determined by whether or not we sense being safe or threatened. We become stuck in patterned behavior that is meant to keep us safe. As adaptive as these advantages may have been for early human being, these strategies are not helpful in most complex relationship situations. If we do not have skills, life seems much more threatening. If we gain the skills we need to negotiate life events, we do not have to respond to life situations with an emotional response. We do not have to run, to fight, to camouflage, or play dead. The second perceptual system we have available to us should help us to become clearer about our life circumstances, but do feelings really help to guide us toward a logical conclusion?

SUBJECTIVITY

As we move from being an infant to being young children, we begin to have feelings. The feelings we have are simply the product of whether or not we sense being safe. If we are safe, we may sense love, happiness, joy, or other feelings associated with safety. If we are threatened, we may sense fear, hate, hurt, guilt, or other feelings associated with being threatened. Some of our feelings reinforce the sense of well-being, while some of our feelings reinforce a sense of not being okay. We can easily see how feelings should help us to determine whether or not our world is safe or threatening. It is also easy to see that if our feelings are based on an inaccurate assessment of our world that we could be using our feelings to make decisions that are not in our best interest. Focusing on our feelings as our primary guide for what we should do increases the likelihood that our feelings will be more intense. Feelings, no matter how volatile or intense, do eventually dissipate in spite of what our behavior is. We may find our Selves having made a major decision about a life situation based on how we felt at a moment in time only to deeply regret the decision later.

We can begin to see that when our parents do not allow us to explore either due to under-protecting us or over-protecting us, we do not gain skills to help us do anything but rely on our emotions and our feelings to make life decisions. It is interesting that when we are attempting to make life decisions, one of the first questions we ask our Selves is how do we feel about it. Does this really seem like the most helpful focus we could have?

As we transfer our feelings from our parents to others outside our families, we need skills beyond those afforded us by emotions and feelings. Constantly relying on our feelings and emotions as guides, we will react to everyone we meet. When we are purely reacting, our behavior is not based on what we think is in our best interest: instead our behavior is based on what another person is doing. Our behavior is based on our emotional assessment if we are safe or threatened by the person to whom we are relating. We lose our sense of Self. When we think about what it is like to experience that we have lost our Selves by attending to a relationship instead of our own needs, can we see that this formula leads us only one direction? Mired in our feelings and emotions, we have no way to use our third perceptual system to help us make life decisions.

OBJECTIVITY

We can begin to collect facts fairly early in life. We cannot, however, make sense of how these facts fit together. Think about when we are in grade school. We begin to learn numbers. We learn facts about these numbers but not advanced relationships these numbers have to one another. As we get older, we begin to understand how these numbers can interrelate. From deeper understanding, we begin to learn how to think about numbers on a more abstract level and how math can impact our lives. We gain a broader view from which we can now use math in a highly effective manner to help us in our day-to-day lives. We engage in this same process when we learn how to research, reason, and reflect from our families.

Now think about learning math from someone who does not know math him/her Self. Does that sound like a good idea? Would you entrust a class of children to a teacher who had never had a math course? When we fail to see this process as a natural progression toward maturation in our children, we can sense threat about what is happening. From a threatened position, we may react in ways that do not help our children to gain the skills necessary to make well-thought-out decisions. When our children are teens, we seem particularly sensitive to how our children relate to us. We may have missed cues up to this point that our children had not learned the skills necessary to negotiate successfully. But, at the time when we anticipate that our children will become more independent, we may see the first signs that they do not have the skills to do so. It is as a young adult that we will become most aware of our Selves in relation to our skills for independent functioning. That is when we are expected to begin to function without the assistance of others.

Our parents' understanding of what is happening is critical to us. It does matter. >From our parents teaching us---most likely inadvertently----we can become stuck in a state of awareness and response that will not allow us to access our ability to research, reason, or reflect. Without these skills, we are not as apt to successfully negotiate relationships as adults. At the very time we are expected to function more independently, if we are unable to do so, the sense of threat can intensify to a state of "dysfunction". Our reaction to life challenges can vary from a state of not being able to tell the difference between reality and what is made up to drug use, to promiscuity, to being unable to maintain a relationship for any length of time, to depression, to anxiety attacks, and so on. Without the ability to research, reason, and reflect we may make life decisions that make little to no logical sense and are no more than a series of behaviors designed to secure our "safety". If we have heard the myth that an intimate relationship can provide a haven of "safety", we may find our Selves in a series of relationships involvements that end in unhappy states.

These involvements may lead to more threat than safety. Such a process can result in life long patterns that totally dumbfound us as to how we got to the end point where our lives have been more disappointment than joy, more isolation than connection, and more confusing than sensible. The most interesting aspect of reaching this point in our lives is that we have the capacity to lead very different lives.

NURTURE

The formation of a meaningful connection to our parents that gives us the resource of support we need to establish an independent, functionally mature Self begins from our birth. We will learn from our parents through our daily experiences. Our parents teach us to perceive and interpret what we experience as either threatening or safe. Based on what we learn, we will establish life long patterns that we will follow: in other words, we can embrace myths about relationships and never be able to shake our Selves free of these myths. Without more mature levels of function, we could never even know that we are making life decisions based on myth.

The earliest learning that we do about the degree of safety or the degree of threat in a relationship hinges on our needs for survival being met through our relationship with our caregivers. If we are totally denied resources for our survival, we die. If our needs for survival are met based on our own awareness of our needs and behavioral expression of our needs, and an adult realistically meets those needs, then we will perceive of and interpret relationships as safe. The likelihood as an adult of being able to form and maintain relationships in which each person experiences safety increases greatly. Any degree of over-protection or under-protection or over-valuing or under-valuing of a child by a parent diminishes that child's opportunity to learn the skills necessary to relate with a realistic assessment of threat or safety. When a parent over-protects or under-protects a child, it is due to that parent misperceiving and misinterpreting threat or safety. When a parent over-values or under-values a child, it is due to that parent misperceiving and misinterpreting the degree of threat or safety that the child presents to the parent's life. As simplistic as it sounds, the quality of our adult relationships are determined in our bassinettes and in our sand boxes. We may not be able to see the results until later, but the learning of skills occurs as children interface with their parents. This is true for all parents.

At the time that a parent over-protects a child, it is usually not from making a well-informed decision. It is from using the sense of threat or safety that a parent has had from childhood himself or herself. When a parent has not learned that the world is a safe place, the automatic reaction is to protect his or her child. Over-protecting means that we take some kind of action to prevent our child from being exposed to the situation that we see as threatening. When we do not encounter an experience, we cannot learn to take care of our Selves when this situation presents itself. That means that we will be stuck with avoiding the situation in the future or having to deal with it without the adaptive skills in place. We are not like bacteria: we cannot mutate to solve our dilemma. We must actually use our processes of thinking to successfully adapt to our life dilemmas. The sense of threat and fear drive this entire process; that means that we cannot engage thought. When threat and fear are our experience, we cannot think. We can only react with the few behaviors available to us. Our parents seeing us as in danger means that we will learn to be protective of our Selves. We can become shy, withdrawn, uncertain of our Selves, and fearful all based on someone else believing that the world is a dangerous place. Our life experiences can dwindle to living very minimal lives.

Being over-protected means that we must turn to someone else to protect us. When we do not learn skills, then we must rely on others who have those skills to take care of us. If we think of relationships as safe, then we have some place to turn, although when we must rely on our Selves, we will probably find the world a very threatening place to be. If we do not see relationships as safe, then we have no place to turn for comfort or for resources. We are isolated and alone. Being isolated and alone and fearful is a combination that can impact our relationships with others in very negative ways. When we depend on someone else to function for us, we use their life energy to devote to us, and we lose our own ability to function for our Selves. We must constantly watch the relationship and be sensitive to any potential for disruption. Everyone loses their own functioning. Some parents, however, experience parenting as a threat to Self.

For parents who sense that Self is threatened by the demands of parenting, these parents may push their children out into the world in a way that under-protects these children. The same outcome of having not enough skills to find the world a safe place happens. These children are thrust into the world unprepared. They have the same choices as anyone who is stuck in an emotional reaction to relationships. Reactions range from collapsing to pretending to be tougher than the person really is. Imagine being asked to negotiate adult issues as a child who is ill prepared to manage. Children may learn some skills from trial and error, or they may learn skills from other adults. The support system that they need to function adaptively to the challenges of life is absent. We can think about people we have known who seem invisible as a way to not have to relate. We do not hear their wishes, we do not hear about their needs, because they sense a high degree of threat in expressing these, if they know what they need or want. For children who pretend to be more of a Self than they really are, these children must avoid real, intimate relationships. If someone tries to get close to them, they cannot allow this, because their pretense will be discovered. We see children who may be very active and very involved who fall into this category. The pretense is so effective; it is difficult to know that their individual experience of life is very different than they act like it is. Parents may also over-value or under-value their child.

When a child is over-valued, the child never receives accurate feedback about the skills they are developing. This child may assume that they have the skills needed to survive and find out when they attempt to leave home that their skills are inadequate. We can hear the parents of these children tell them how wonderful they are even if what they did does not measure up. The parent is assuming that the child is too fragile to hear the "truth", so instead they lie. Soon the child does not know what the "truth" is. Their sense of reality is distorted. When our sense of reality is distorted, the world may seem very frightening. It is near impossible to know what to do if we do not know what accurate information is. If we stopped to think about an analogy, if we were to teach a child a language made up of gibberish, the child would have no language to negotiate the world. The child would face a fair degree of threat to getting their needs met as an independent adult. We paralyze our children when we do not give them accurate feedback. Moving from a position of always being pleasing to others to not knowing how to please another person is threatening. The more realistic the parent is about the child's capabilities helps the child to gain skills and use tools that are factually effective in negotiating the world. On the opposite side of over-valuing a child is the parent who under-values a child.

The under-valued child soon learns that he or she will never measure up. This can be difficult for the child, as a pattern of failure becomes what the child expects of the world. A child who is under-valued is not taught the skill he or she needs to master the world as an adult, because the parent assumes the child is not capable. The parent may view the child as having some kind of inability to learn, and as such, does not try to teach the child. The child simply is never exposed to what the child needs to become independent. No parent ever purposefully sets out to raise a child who is unable to function. All parents do the best they can based on what they know. We all depend on our parents to teach us, and what our parents teach us is all we know to teach our children.

What this means is that **learning whether or not the world is a threatening place or a safe place based on the facts IS A MULTIGENERATIONAL PROCESS.** In other words, all of us learn from our parents. It is the only place we can learn. Our parents are impacted by the parameters that society defines. And, our parents are also impacted by the parameters defined by Nature. It is easy to be unable to see this emotional process being passed along from generation to generation. The process can get buried under the mountain of events: we get so focused on the content; we simply do not see the patterns. Or, we do not know our families well enough to gather the information needed to reason and reflect. Not knowing our families well enough or not seeing the patterns because we are so focused on the content are both strong indicators that we are caught in reacting to life events from an emotional perceptual system.

Gathering facts about our families and what their emotional reactions to life were is helpful to us. With these facts, we can begin to piece the puzzle together. From understanding, we can take into account the experience of the other person involved. This allows us to make informed decisions based on information about everyone in the system. The objective is not to please everyone but to respect that we are committed to our relationships as well as to our Selves. When we step back from what is happening in our life, we can begin to see that our families for generations have faced similar issues and passes along patterned solutions to us. These solutions may have proven highly ineffective for a number of years, but what else can our parents teach us?

We can see how this multigenerational process plays itself out with the following example.

John: Over-protected	Ann: Under-protected
RUN: John avoids any situation that is perceived as unknown. Should John try a "novel" situation, his sense of threat escalates to the point that he cannot access his ability to gather information, understand how information fits together, and reflect on how the situation impacts all the individuals involved. John will most likely experience failure without being able to think. Once he fails, he has reinforced that he should avoid novel situations and needs the protection of someone else.	RUN: Ann senses extreme threat when she attempts to be close to another person. She senses that if she is open with another person about her real self and her fears, she will not be accepted and will have to admit that she is alone. As a result, Ann never allows anyone to really get to know her. She does not talk about what is important to her but waits to hear what the other person says is important to them. Then she merely agrees with them.
FIGHT: John may engage in an argument to free himself of someone else trying to tell him what to do. His sense of Self is threatened if someone else is telling him what to do, however, John has not developed the skills necessary to do what he wants to do. The sense of threat bolstered by his anger, he does not think through what he would need to do to be successful. He subsequently fails, which is further evidence that he needs protection.	FIGHT: Ann blames another person when anything goes wrong without ever stopping to assess if she had a part in what happened. As she blames others, she engages in heated arguments with them in which she stays on the offensive, therefore, never allowing another person to bring up any way in which she may have been responsible.

PLAY DEAD: John may tell others that something does not matter to him when it really does. He may sense a great deal of threat in attempting to have something when he knows he does not have the skills to attain it. He may be able to cut-off altogether from his feelings and genuinely not be aware of any feeling but acceptance of the situation.	PLAY DEAD: Ann never expresses any need for anyone to help her. She does have a lot of people around her but she does this based on other's needs. Ann secretly is very depressed about her sense of isolation but never allows anyone to know about this depression. People view Ann as always being happy.
CAMOUFLAGE: John may use the strategy of never trying to do anything without the support of his parents or without getting direction from his parents. His parents may be able to always help him to the point that his inadequacies are never known. He can, therefore, never fail and never have to reckon with the fact that he has not learned the skills essential to be on his own.	CAMOUFLAGE: Ann pretends to never be scared of a situation. She may be terrified but denies that she is anxious about a situation. As a result, she tried to keep such situations to a minimum. She will not try new things unless she has some assurances that she will succeed.

We all know people like John and Ann. We cannot alter our states of awareness of our Selves nor come up with solutions to the problems we have to deal with because of our immaturity, unless we work to unlearn old patterns of relating. This requires that we gather facts about our pasts, understand how nature has worked with nurture to bring us to the point where we are, and then learn to consider others who are important to us as we make life decisions. We must realize that just like our ancestors on the open plains, we will experience discomfort as we try to understand our worlds from a different frame of reference. We must shed our Selves of myths and recognize our Selves as separate people in intimate relationships. Until we do that, we are caught in our repetitive responses for the duration. It is never too late to begin to research, reason, and reflect. Pat is the perfect example of grappling with our awareness of our Selves and our responses to others based on this awareness.

Pat was a 58-year-old woman who had been married and divorced three times. She was living alone for the first time in her life and found living alone to be difficult. As she struggled with life circumstances she did not know how to handle, she found herself eating for comfort and over-spending to make herself feel better. Her solutions soon became life problems that now were added to her list of relationship disasters. Pat saw herself as a failure in every area of her life. Her job provided her little reward and demanded she work very hard. Her home was of little comfort to her, and she found herself letting it go. Soon the life energy required to straighten out her life seemed like more than she could cope with. Her friends were kind and caring people, but she oftentimes sensed being less than they were. She saw them as involved and satisfied with their lives. It was hard for Pat to continue to be engaged in friendships. She became more and more isolated.

One night Pat decided to go to a movie. She was in line at the ticket counter and noticed that the man in front of her had dropped a five-dollar bill. She bent over to pick it up for him, and as she started to hand it to him, she noticed he did not have on a wedding band. He thanked Pat for picking up the bill, and they began to chat. He was going to see a different movie from Pat, and they compared notes about the movies they had selected to see. When they reached the ticket counter, they said goodbyes. As Pat entered the theatre, she saw him at the counter buying some refreshments. Although she had not planned to buy refreshments, she decided to get in line behind him, so she could continue to chat with him. Pat thought that they had a lot in common, and she did not want to pass up the opportunity to learn his name.

As she approached the counter, he turned and spoke to her. They engaged in conversation once again, and as he got his refreshments he turned to say goodbye again. As he left, he suggested he might run into her after the movie. Pat left the refreshment line, and went to check on the schedule for when his movie would end. Pat was pleased, because his movie ended ten minutes after the movie she was seeing. Pat went to see the movie for which she had purchased a ticket, but she found herself spending most of her time wondering if he "really" like her and if she was making up the interest she thought he expressed in her.

The movie ended. Pat went straight to the restroom where she touched up her makeup and applied fresh lipstick. Then she tried to decide where she could position herself, so that it would appear that they were once again casually bumping into one another. She decided that she could pretend to be leaving the restroom just as he was passing by. She waited a little to the side of the doorway and heard some people discussing the movie. She decided to step into the aisle and started searching for him. As soon as she saw him, she waved, so he would notice her.

He came over and started to tell her about the movie he had seen. Pat made sure to ask lots of questions about the movie and suggested they have a cup of coffee while they talked. Soon they were sitting together discussing the movies they had seen. One topic led to another and finally he asked for her number. Pat gave him her e-mail address, because it seemed safer to her. They departed, and Pat drove home immediately to wait for the e-mail.

On the way home, she called two of her friends and asked them what they thought. Each of them responded warmly to her excitement and encouraged her that he had indeed seemed interested. By the end of the evening, Pat had already decided where they could go on their first date. She looked his name and number up in the telephone directory and called a friend to ask if she knew the neighborhood. Her friend knew someone who lived in that neighborhood. Pat asked her to call her friend and find out if she knew Dan. Her friend called her back and informed her that he was single, lived alone, and was a really nice person. Pat knew that she had been destined to meet Dan. It was fate. She stayed up late on the computer waiting for his e-mail, but nothing arrived. She finally fell asleep late.

The next morning when she checked the computer and no e-mail had arrived, Pat began to explain in her head why he had been unable to e-mail her immediately. She made us several different explanations as to why he had not called. All of her explanations seemed reasonable, but she called a friend to check out what her friend thought. Her friend assured her that her explanations were reasonable. Pat got ready for work a little early, because she wanted to drive by his house on the way to work to see where he lived.

She carefully checked as she neared his home to make certain that he was not out where he might see her. His home was nice. It appeared that he enjoyed to garden as he had many plants around his house. That was good, because Pat really enjoyed yard work if someone were able to work outdoors with her. She had lamented many times that her yard would look quite different if she had someone who enjoyed yard work with her. All of a sudden, Pat started thinking about working in Dan's yard with him. In a heartbeat, she had herself living with Dan in his house.

It was difficult for Pat to focus on her work wondering if she would have an e-mail when she got home. She drove a little over the speed limit to get home and was rewarded with an e-mail waiting on her computer. Pat was a little breathless with anticipation as she opened the e-mail. She had not been mistaken: he did like her. His e-mail was fairly long and chatty. He talked about having gone to work out after the movie at a gym near his house. Pat suddenly worried that if he liked to work out that he might not be interested in her with her weight problem. She resolved on the spot to get in shape.

She responded to his e-mail and found herself making suggestive comments to him as she wrote responses to things he said. Pat was excited about what she saw as a probable relationship between them. Pat had not thought of herself as being involved with anyone. Now she knew that she was quite lonely and needed someone to complete her life and help her to correct her life circumstances. Pat sort of suggested something that they could do together. She made enough of an offer to see if he were interested but not enough of an offer to make it look as if she were too interested.

After Pat responded to his e-mail, she drove over to the workout center where Dan said he went and asked about membership fees. She spent money she did not have but justified spending the money to help her with her health. From there, she went and bought workout clothes so she would feel good about going to the gym. She stopped on the way home and went for a long walk. When she returned home, she checked her e-mail. He had responded, and she was on top of the world. She wrote right back mentioning to him the long walk she had taken on the way home hoping he would suggest that they go on a walk.

Dan did suggest that they go for a walk. They met the next day at a park after Pat finished work. They walked for a couple of hours and talked non-stop. As they left each other, Dan gave her a kiss. It was not just a peck on the cheek. Pat knew now that he was very interested in her. As she drove home, she wondered at which house they would live and how their children would get along when holidays came around. In Pat's mind, they were married.

When Dan called next, Pat responded very warmly. After all, she was safe with Dan, because he really liked her and wanted a relationship with her. She had analyzed every word he had spoken on their walk, discussed it with two of her friends who agreed with her, and was certain that this was the relationship she had been waiting for. Dan called the next day and asked if he could drop by for a few minutes.

Pat rushed around trying to tidy her house before he arrived. She put on her most flattering outfit and was barely ready when the doorbell rung. When she opened the door, she was taken by how handsome he was. He was smiling and was obviously glad to see her. Within an hour of his arrival, they were in bed making "love". He stayed for a couple of hours, had some coffee and had to leave. Pat called all of her friends and told them how wonderful the relationship was. She was convinced that he was in love with her and that they would be married within the year. She told her friends about their plans to travel: Dan had told her about the trips he had planned.

Two weeks passed with no word from Dan. Pat was beside herself with worry. She went over every detail of what had happened between the time they met and the present. She tried, desperately, to figure out what she had done or said that had made him get distant with her. She called her friends and went over all the details again, asking them if they could figure out what she did wrong. Then, Pat decided she would go to the workout center and eventually she would see him again. She justified that he just needed a nudge. Her friends were beginning to tell her that they thought Dan was using her, but Pat was convinced that he really cared for her. She saw him as somehow unable to express his true feelings for her.

Pat started working out. Working out was good for her, so she had an excuse for running into him. She did within a couple of weeks. He was very kind to her and did not mention their love-making. She flirted with him in an obvious manner, but he left without mentioning seeing her again. Pat was quite upset. She called all of her friends asking what they thought she should do. Each of them gave the same advice. Don't bother with this man. Pat thought that they just had not seen how he had looked at her and how he had touched her when they were in bed. She looked for a reason to call him, and finally she decided to call and confront him with how he was treating her. If they could just talk about it, she knew they could work it out between them.

Dan answered, and Pat made up an excuse about why she was calling him. She had some question about how the health club worked and needed to ask someone who had been there for awhile. Dan answered her question and was very warm and friendly. Then Pat asked why he had not called. Dan told Pat that he had gathered from what she had said as he was leaving that she really wasn't interested in him calling her. She explained in no uncertain terms that he had definitely misunderstood what she had said. She made it clear that she definitely wanted to see him again. They talked for a couple of hours and hung up again, without Dan mentioning seeing her again.

Pat again called all her friends and let them know that they had been wrong. Dan was a really nice person who just had misunderstood something she had said. Now that she had corrected his misunderstanding, things would be fine. She knew he would call soon, and they could proceed forward with forming a life together. Pat was very excited.

Days passed. Days turned into a couple of weeks. Pat was beside herself. Each day she called her friends and poured her heart out to them. They all gave the same advice. This man was not a nice person: stop dreaming. Then she bumped into Dan at a place he had told her that he often walked.

Dan had been out of town. He was very glad to see her. She invited him over for coffee. They made love again. He stayed for a couple of hours and was very loving to her. Pat was certain that the relationship was definitely back on track. Do we have to go any further with this description?

Everyone but Pat could see what was happening. Had Pat been able to look back at her life, she would have seen several patterns that were repeating. As a child Pat was adored by her mother and was very over-protected. She had one older sibling who was male and much older than she was. Her mother had doted on her while she was growing up. Pat learned few life skills to take care of her Self. Her mother made sure she had everything she needed without Pat ever having to tell her mother what she needed or wanted. Her clothes were laid out every morning, her mother involved her in all the right social activities, and her mother was very involved in all her school events. Pat had the perfect life. When Pat became a teenager, she started to express an interest in boys. Her mother was horrified and forbade Pat to go out with boyfriends.

All of Pat's friends were going out with guys, and Pat saw her Self as something being wrong with her. She began sneaking out of the house against her mother's wishes, and her relationship with her parents began to deteriorate. Eventually things were so strained between them that Pat stopped going home altogether. Pat had no one to look after her, so she turned to the boy she was dating. Within a short period of time, she was married and pregnant with her first child. Suddenly Pat realized that the man she married had a serious drinking problem and was seeing other women. She was extremely upset and felt justified to return home to her parents with her child. Within a short period of time, the demands of her parents on her to be a respectable mother and stay home with them resulted in several arguments. She had been dating a man against her parent's wishes and decided that he would take care of her. They married. She left her daughter with her parents as her parents insisted this was in the daughter's best interest to get her marriage off to a good start. Eventually Pat's daughter would move in with her and her husband. But, what eventually happened was that Pat discovered her second husband was seeing another woman.

The story continues. What we see is a pattern of not being aware that Pat was a separate person from others. She assumed that if she had positive feelings and sensed being safe that the men she was meeting had the exact same needs and wants as she did. She responded by committing to a relationship before she really knew these men, although in retrospect she always had evidence that they were not who they pretended to be.

Pat is 58 years old. She has decided to work to change how she has managed her life. As she has done so, it has been important for Pat to gather facts about the threats that she faces. She is working on a physical exercise program going to the gym regularly. She has consulted with a senior volunteer about her finances and is more aware of her tendency to spend money to help her to deal with her emotions and feelings. Pat has been collecting information about her family to help her to understand how her parents became so concerned and overly protective. She has joined a couple of groups that have members who are more like she is: single and living alone. From gathering facts about her life, Pat is seeing patterns that are helping her to pause when she is in a position in which she senses a need to react to a situation.

Pat is slowing down. She is trying to be more realistic about what happens between men and her. When she talks to her friends, she tries to listen to their feedback and not hear what they are saying as some kind of threat to what she wants. Pat seems more settled. Pat finds herself pleasantly surprised at how easy it has been to manage her Self differently as she is able to use new ideas to see how emotional process impacts her life. When Pat senses a strong feeling, she automatically stops making any major decisions until she has had an opportunity to think about the situation in front of her. She reports she has many more options than she knew she had.

In reference to Dan, Pat understands that she is not responsible for Dan's behavior. She has stopped asking her Self the repetitious questions of what has she done wrong to drive him away. She knows that a serious relationship between them is unlikely to happen. She is starting to date other people. As she does, she is staying as factual as she can about what behavior means. Pat seems much more content with her life when she is aware of the facts, understands how she has created patterns in her relationships, and sees how others have played a part in the outcome of her life. Life is different now for Pat. All her problems have not evaporated, but she sees alternatives that were not available to her before. Her ability to think has given her a new level of adaptive strategies from which to draw when life presents challenges.

Pat's life is not unlike our's. We fail to be aware of our Selves as separate from others. If we sense a relationship as familiar, we plunge headlong into it without gathering the facts, without seeing how the facts fit into a pattern, and without stopping to really consider who the other person really is. We make extreme assumptions and then act as if we are appalled when things are the way we pretended they were.

We engage in myth. The light flickers on our faces: not from our fireplaces but from our televisions. We set with walls of isolation between us. The walls come from the myth that we can be one with one another, forsaking our Selves and then be happy and content creatures. We expect the impossible. We have the capacities to be more for our Selves and to be more for each other. We can let go of myth. Facts that help us to piece together our lives to help us make sense of what happens to us change our perspective. We can see the part that we play in how our lives work out. We can see the part that others play. And then, we can make choices that keep us safe and allow us to explore intimacy.

END OF CHAPTER WORK

Review the chapter and find the main ideas that seemed to make us think. How could these ideas be helpful to us?

A family chart is oftentimes a useful tool as we work to understand how we use human nature based on what our families teach us. As we make this chart, it is usually most helpful to gather facts about how each person generally behaves when threatened as well as each person behaves when safe. What patterns do we see as we look at this chart? How can we use patterns our families have formed to help us in our daily lives with our spouses?

What myths would we say are interfering with our intimate relationships? How are these myths interfering with our relationships? What would it take for us to alter these myths?

CHAPTER FOUR

Basic Way We Relate #2
People React to Each Other

Cruising along the coast of Ecuador in the Pacific Ocean we land on the Galapagos Islands. We begin to explore and find that the animals on the islands seem as interested in us as we seem in them. These animals seem to sense no fear of us. They do not run. They do not hide. They sense no need to escape. They do not attack. They do not defend territory. They sense no need to fight. As we explore, so do they. Their behavior amazes us, and we revel in the exquisite experience of an intimate encounter with a species far from our own kind.

These animals do not behave, as we would expect if we were using our experiences with encounters with animals in other parts of the world as our baseline. The reason for the "strangeness" of their behavior is not that they are less "smart" as their cousins in other parts of the world. The reason for their behavior is that they have not learned to sense threat from other species. On Galapagos, predation is not a real fear. Fear is not a constant and steady influence on behavior. The animals have not learned behaviors associated with the fear for one's life. We can, therefore, experience a degree of intimacy with these animals that is impossible with other species in other parts of the world.

If we were half way around the earth in Africa, our encounters with others species would be much less intimate. We would, instead of approaching animals to sit next to them as we watch their off-spring suckle, keep our distance and prepare to have greater distance between our selves and their selves should the animals sense danger and react to protect themselves. The need to protect self from predators creates wariness in animals. Intimate encounters cannot be a part of this formula. These animals are surrounded by the threat of predation. As a result, their behaviors are grossly different than the animals with which we have interacted on Galapagos. They have learned to sense fear, to be wary of others of a different species. Discriminating between friend and foe requires a greater deal of life energy in Africa than is required on Galapagos. A sense of alertness expends energy but saves lives. In Africa, those who are able to react almost immediately stand a higher chance of survival than those who react slowly. Being on guard instead of being curious pays off. We react to these animals with a sense of threat: we keep our distance. Calm and fear lead to immensely different behaviors. Animals, like our selves, assess the environment for threat and react accordingly. Behavioral patterns become established based on the intensity of this sense of threat and fear. That is a fact for all species.

Fact About Intimate Behavior #2:

People React to Each Other

Turning to our own self, we find similar behavioral patterns. Some of us have learned a high degree of alertness to the possibility of emotional hurt and have become wary of our relationships ending or of our relationships asking us to be close and connected. Some of us are calmer about the degree of threat we sense as we relate to others. It is those persons who sense calm in relationships who are most apt to find and maintain close, intimate contact. We can explore; we can be close; we can "risk". When we sense threat, we do not explore but stay in a protective mode. We cannot be close without eliciting in ourselves a deep sense of threat that results in automatic responses to the relationship. We cannot risk, because our sense of fear gives us only four behavioral options: we run, we fight, we play dead or we camouflage.

Learning plays the same role for us in how we sense relating to others as it does for the animals on Galapagos and in Africa. As Nature has given us protective strategies that function automatically to provide instant protection, nurture has given us the strategy of discriminating between what is dangerous and what is safe. Nurture provides us this strategy though learning from our families. It is the interaction between Nature and Nurture that will determine the behavioral strategies we use dominantly. From this dominant selection of a protective strategy, we establish patterns in our relationships. Most of the time, all of this happens to us without us being aware of it. Not knowing leaves us stuck in relationship patterns that can spiral us downward into deep levels of dysfunction. Knowing about Nature and Nurture, however, gives us two points of intervention to make our lives different from the past. This knowledge gives us hopes that we can change our bedrooms from the African plains to the Galapagos Islands. Would that be a difference you might enjoy?

NATURE

We tend to think of our natures as something we cannot change. And, maybe change is indeed not the appropriate word we should use when we think about making a difference in our lives. A word that offers more realistic hope is management. Management of our nature's sounds a lot more likely to achieve than change. The reason that management is more realistic is that #1. We are talking about changing adaptive strategies that have helped all other successful forms of life to succeed. If something works, it may be important to not get rid of it. The second reason that management is a more realistic goal is that expecting to alter something that has been a part of all life seems like an extremely tall order. If we are not realistic, we set our Selves up to fail. Failure usually promotes a sense of the world not being safe, and then we are engaged in an emotional response that cannot help us to access the tools we need to solve problems.

The tools needed to solve almost any problem lie in the upper portion of our skulls. It is the part of our brain that gathers and processes facts and that allows us to consider other people. These three functions offer us the most effective problem-solving strategies available. So, what stops us from using these strategies to solve our problems?

71

Human perceptual systems work in interesting ways. It is important to understand how these systems work. The facts about how human perceptual systems work encourage us to stop and think versus accepting that we know exactly what we are doing. We can end up with three divorces and still plod along following the same strategies for relationships that we used before. It is not that we believe something is suddenly fixed: it is that we have no other hope except to try and try again. Knowing how we perceive information helps us to know that we are fallible. It gives us permission to re-think our knowledge in a way that does not create a sense of threat. When we believe we do not know what we are doing we are threatened.

As we receive information from our environments, our brain begins to scan previous files for information experienced before. The first level of assessment is to ascertain if our environment presents a threat. If we are safe, we are free to relate freely. It is the period of time that we can gain skills and formulate effective solutions to life problems. If this is the case, then how come we still find our Selves in age-old pickles? Well the answer is that our brains scrunch data and file the scrunched data into files that might match without carefully making certain that the scrunched data belongs in the file. If we have an experience in the past that is remotely similar to the experience we are having, our brain tells us that it is the same experience. We are, therefore, very apt to behave in the same way that we have behaved in the past. We do not see the situation as novel, so we do not know to access our processes for research, reason, and reflection. This is critical information.

Obviously, scrunching data makes adaptive sense. Otherwise, we would be so encumbered trying to understand each daily life event that we would be unable to function. Our species would not have survived the dangerous times in which we lived had our brains paid attention to moderate variations. Only variations in detail that are major catch our attention. What this does to us, however, is leave us extremely vulnerable to error. We are *likely* on a daily bases to draw conclusions that are erroneous. If this is the case, we might want to be more careful making decisions about our relationships on a daily bases. We might ask our Selves the question, is the conclusion I am drawing about my partner accurate? Instead we spend little time asking this question.

An example may help us to see how little time we spend re-thinking our relationship behaviors. Jim was divorced from his second wife. They had three children, and he had taken custody of the children. Janice did not want custody of the children, and her inconsistent behavior resulted in many and intense arguments between Jim and Janice. He sought help in dealing with his ex-wife. The following situation happened and illustrates what we are talking about in terms of rarely stopping to think about what we assume we know. Jim came to the therapy session with the following report.

Jim had a situation at work in which a corporation had purchased the company for which he worked. The word was that top management would be evaluating middle-level management and be asking people to leave who were not contributing meaningfully to the team. Jim was notified he would be presenting the same week that he had also scheduled a meeting with his ex-wife. The meeting with his ex-wife was extremely important to determine custody patterns. The children had adjustment problems each time they saw their mother, and she had taken them to a couple of inappropriate parties. The meeting with work was scheduled for Wednesday. The meeting with his ex-wife was scheduled for Friday.

Jim went to his therapy session with the following report. Jim had spent hours preparing for the meeting at work. He had gathered all the data available and had designed a plan to help higher management understand how the data indicated the importance of the research his division had been doing. He demonstrated how each person on his team was integral to the success of the project and showed them how the project was vital to the health of the company. Jim did an excellent job and had found out that his division would continue its work uninterrupted. Then Jim reported about his meeting with his ex-wife.

The meeting with his ex-wife ended with them having an intense argument and her making threats to take the children if he did not agree to the financial settlement she wanted.
She demanded to see the children more frequently and would not agree to supervised visits. Jim was very upset and did not know what in the

world he was going to do. Jim's therapist asked him how much time he had spent on getting ready for the meeting with his ex-wife. Jim reported that he had done nothing to get ready for the meeting with his ex-wife, because he knew her.

This is a great example of how easily we dismiss the need to think before we engage in important relationship discussions. We assume that we do not need to think, because we already know how we need to handle situations with our partners. Had Jim spent some time gathering the facts that were pertinent to their meeting, reasoned about a plan that would be helpful to the children, and put himself in the place of his ex-wife to try to see her point of view, this meeting could have turned out much more differently.

We cannot rely on what we know, because what we know is not helping us in our intimate relationships with each other. Something stops us from pursuing a different way of understanding our relationships with each other. Our brains assess for threat, automatically. It is the very first thing that happens, and it is instant. If our brains cannot recognize the situation in front of us as being even remotely familiar, then we are alerted to think. If we are alerted to think, and we cannot make sense of what we are experiencing, then we sense threat. Once we sense threat, we cannot engage our neo-cortex to research, reason, and reflect. At that point, we seem to accept any reasonable explanation. *Then,* we do not need to research, reason, or reflect in the future if the situation we are experiencing is even remotely familiar to our brain. We recognize the situation as something about which we know and behave accordingly. If our behavior results in a relationship problem, we do not stop to question the way we understand the situation: we try to figure out what went wrong or start asking what is wrong with the other person. We are prone to error.

EMOTIONS

The most natural tendency when we sense we are not safe is to take protective measures to ensure our safety. As we take these measures, we believe strongly that we have done the "right" thing. That means that we are not stopping to ask our Selves if we are accurate in our assessment or even accurate in our perception. We react to the sense of threat much too quickly in many instances.

For example, Mary had remarried and found soon after the marriage that the man she had married was not who she thought he was. He had a history of using drugs, and he was unkind to her children. Her friends urged her to get out of the relationship immediately. Mary took measures to make sure that her husband had minimal contact with her children, but she did not immediately file for a divorce. Mary decided to not leave the relationship until she could understand how come she had gotten into the relationship. Once Mary was able to research, reason, and reflect, she did opt to leave the marriage. The process of research, reason, and reflection helped Mary to see that she had married to help her deal with the threat she sensed in being on her own and totally responsible for raising her children. Mary also discovered a lot more about her Self. She left with a clearer understanding about what prompted her to get involved with this man to begin with and had clear ideas about what she needed to do to help her Self to become more independent. Because we make a mistake does not mean that the mistake poses a threat to us. Mistakes can be rich in learning potential. But, for mistakes to help us learn lessons, we must research, reason, and reflect.

To live in a relationship like living on Galapagos, we must research, reason, and reflect. It is when we sense safety and are accurate in our assessment that we can be meaningfully connected to another human being. Feelings can be rich, and we can experience emotions, but we do not react based on our emotions and our feelings.

SUBJECTIVITY

Feelings in intimate relationships are given lots of attention. When we are making major decisions in our relationships, we ask our Selves how we feel about the situation. Looking at Mary's situation described above can help us to understand how using our feelings may not be in our best interests.

When Mary met Mark, she was on her own raising her two children. She found it difficult to make ends meet financially, but more importantly, she was concerned that she was not providing a family atmosphere for her children. Mark had been married before, and he handled his own uncertainty in life by pretending to know exactly what he was doing in every situation. However, Mark had just gotten word that he was about to lose his position would be terminated in six months due to a lay off planned by the plant. He had met Mary about two months prior to receiving notice about his job. He had been very attracted to her, but Mark had made a point of not getting involved with anyone. Mark had a history of using drugs intermittently. He did not want anyone to interfere with his drug use, and he certainly did not want anyone in the community to know about his drug use. He had managed to live in the same town for a few years without anyone knowing. Mark had moved to this town, because in the last town he had lived, his work had found out about his drug use and had made his job miserable until he resigned.

Mark needed someone who could help him through this difficult period. Mary owned her own business. The business was stable, but Mary constantly worried that the business would fail. Mark gave her some advice about the business when they started dating. Mark saw an opportunity to save himself from being unemployed, and he also liked Mary. Mark suggested to Mary that he start helping her with the business. Mary was so relieved that she agreed. Mark was a pillar of support. They became more involved with one another. Mark started spending the night at Mary's home and got along well with the children. Mary began to think that this was the relationship that could make her life complete.

Mark suggested they get married for the sake of the children and form a partnership with the business. As soon as they were married, Mary recognized her mistake. Mark would tell her that he had a meeting to go to, and Mary would see his car at the local bar. Mark started coming home later than he was supposed to, and it was obvious to Mary that he had been using some kind of drugs. The children began to register some complaints that when they were alone with Mark, he was not nice to them.

Mary knew that she had to make some changes, but she also recognized the difficult position she was in. Her home was now in her and Mark's name, and so was her business. She managed to schedule her work, so that Mark was no longer alone with the children. She went to see a therapist to try to begin to cope with what was happening but also to try to understand what had prompted her to marry Mark. As she discovered how her fears had driven her toward what she thought was an answer to make her and the children safe, she recognized some patterns that had been a part of other relationships she had. Mary researched information about her family and learned that the pattern she was in was the same pattern that three generations had followed. Mary could forgive her Self her mistake, and she started taking care action to correct the mistakes she had made.

Mary consulted with professionals to help her with her business and her house as she moved to end the relationship. She was thoughtful in how she moved to end the relationship to minimize the reactivity from Mark. Through this process, Mary looked at the facts that supported that she was capable of independent functioning and providing for her children. She reasoned that she was caught in a pattern that she had not been aware of and had not understood. Then she reflected about what would be best for each person in the system, including Mark. She realized that all the intense feelings she had for Mark were related directly to whether or not she sensed that he was providing her safety or presented a threat to her and her children. As she realized this, she could set her feelings aside and do what needed to be done.

We can use the same process to help our relationships to last. If we research, reason, and reflect, we will come to know whether or not our relationships are viable. If we can research, reason, and reflect prior to making a major life commitment, we can be clearer about selecting a partner who can truly be a life partner. If emotions and feelings are the major determining factor, we can make tremendous errors for which we will pay a price. We will be living in a marriage like life on the plains of Africa. We will be wary and unable to make a meaningful connection that provides us life support.

OBJECTIVITY

Objectivity is a part of our natures as well. It is not the default system we use when we sense we need protection. In order to utilize our objective system to really help us to adapt successfully to the life challenges we face, we must practice thinking. It sounds rather strange to think about practicing thinking, but it is like any other skill we want to learn. We must carefully discipline our Selves to think through important life decisions. It is rare for us not to have the time it takes to think through life choices. Our families are at stake. Our well-being is at stake.

Researching means that we collect facts about our life circumstances. We can do this by forming a person-to-person relationship with our family members. The relationship is not meant as a "fix" for past hurts. It is a relationship built on an interest in really knowing the experience of others in our families. With facts we can move to reason.

Reasoning means that we have a way to understand how the facts fit together. Understanding what threats our families faced and how they faced them gives us some insight into our own behaviors. We learn from our families, and therefore, if we want to know what it is we learned, we must go back to our family members as a source. Our siblings are caught in the same problems as our Selves. They do not have memories of early years, and those memories are critical for us to piece together the view our families have of what happened as we grew up.

Reflection means that we always consider others as we make life decisions. It means that we "put our Selves in the other person's shoes". This is an essential function for any intimate relationship that can provide a family sustenance. Reflection does not mean that we consider our Selves last: considering our Selves first may actually be in the best interest of the other members of our families. Reflection stems from the research and the reasoning that allows us to stand in the other person's shoes. Each step is important, and each step is part of nature. It is how we are nurtured that determines what part of nature rules our lives.

NURTURE

At times we can see how learning from our parents has impacted our intimate relationships. Most of the time, we do not have a clue. We do not have good enough memories of our early years, and few of us have enough of a relationship with our parents to engage in a conversation about how we were raised. It is easy to be stopped from engaging in such a conversation if our parents have any sensitivity at all to what kind of a job they did raising us. Another common barrier to coming to know about our pasts is that our parents are unaware of emotional process themselves and *cannot* help us to gain a deeper understanding. In the past, we have talked about dysfunctional families and blamed our parents for our problems. It is easy to understand how come parents are sensitive to whether or not they have done a "good" job raising us. Most parents want the best for their children, but all parents are limited in how much they know to teach.

When we pause to think about how nature has influenced our parenting, we can easily see that how we perceive and interpret events in our lives has a great deal to do with how we parent our children. When we sense the world as safe, we are freer in allowing our children to explore and, thus, gain skills needed to become responsible, mature, and independent adults. When we sense the world is not safe, we take protective measures that oftentimes inhibit learning the skills we need for independence. When a parent is engaged in protecting a child, minimal life energy will go into research, reason, and reflection about the job of parenting. In other words, when we sense threat as a parent, we are unable to think: we simply react in what we assume is the best interest of our children.

We know that we are prone to err in our perceptions and, therefore, our interpretations. As parents, we have minimal feedback about how we are parenting. When we do get feedback, it often comes in the form of criticism or is delivered in a manner that increases the likelihood that we will sense a threat. The usual time that we get feedback is when our children either achieve an honor or get into trouble. But, these may not be our best gauges about the job we are doing as a parent.

At times, our children are in trouble and are high achievers. At other times our children may be doing okay and end up in a situation in which they are in trouble. Grandparents are not considered reliable to give objective feedback. School systems are curtailed in how they give feedback and what feedback they give based on legal issues in education. Everywhere we look, there are limits about getting feedback. Few of us seek meaningful feedback from our children. Getting reliable feedback that our parenting has been less than effective usually comes at times when it is impossible to change our behaviors to help our children to become more mature or more responsible. It is at this point in time, that if we knew what to do, we would have already done it. Professionals seem extremely limited in helping us to know what to do. So, we do what we have been taught, or we do the opposite of what our parents did, or we do some variation of these two strategies.

Whatever strategies we learn as children, we will take these strategies into adulthood and apply the solutions to the challenges we will face in our intimate relationships. Lauren was a great example of observing her parents marriage and drawing conclusions about what she believed she had learned from them.

Lauren was to be married in June. It was now March, and she and her to be husband were making many plans for the wedding. One of the requirements of the minister who had agreed to perform the ceremony was to provide Lauren and Brad pre-marital counseling. The minister had found over time that such counseling sessions often times helped a couple to identify areas in the relationship that could result in marital unhappiness. Lauren and Brad saw the pre-marital counseling sessions as an obligation they had to comply with in order to have the minister perform the ceremony. Neither of them thought the sessions would reveal to them anything they did not already know about each other.

Lauren was a highly successful financial planner. She had worked hard all the way through college, found a job with a firm immediately after graduation, and had proved herself worthy of the promotions and success she had with her firm. Brad was a very successful attorney who was doing well, but he was not as driven for success as Lauren was. This difference was not a problem for them. Each of them recognized that their drives were different.

During the first counseling session, the minister asked them what they planned to do about having a family. Brad and Lauren had talked about having a family, but they had not talked in any detail. Eventually they had assumed that they would have children, but they had not talked about how they would raise their children. Talking about how they would raise their children seemed very premature to them. The minister asked if one of them would place their career on hold when children were younger, and Brad immediately answered that Lauren would become a stay-at-home mom. He said that his income could allow them to do this, and that children needed a mother at home when they came home from school. Lauren was shocked to hear this come out of Brad's mouth. Nothing was farther from her interest than staying at home to raise children.

Lauren had an immediate reaction. She told Brad it would be a cold day in hell before she would be stuck at home with a house full of children. Brad was stunned by her reaction, and he said he had always assumed that she would want to stay home and raise children to give them a good start. He also went on to say that he could easily provide for the family and that if Lauren did not stay home with the children that she was being selfish. Brad said he believed that children who had a stay-at-home mom stood less chance of getting into trouble.

By the time Brad finished what he had to say, Lauren was extremely angry. She accused Brad of being a narrow-minded sexist man who obviously could care less about her well-being. The situation escalated, and Lauren ended up storming out of the counseling session. Brad sat there after she left and asked the minister what it was that he had done that was so wrong. The minister was not exactly certain what the issues were that had led Lauren to react to what Brad had said. He suggested that Brad give Lauren some time to calm down and start thinking about what had happened. They were scheduled for their next session the next week, but the minister offered to Brad time to talk between this session and the one next week. He also let Brad know that he would make the same offer to Lauren.

When he called Lauren, she was still pretty upset. She indicated that she saw him as agreeing with Brad. Immediately the minister let her know that he was not as concerned about who was "right" as what had led to her strong reactions. He suggested they get together and see if they could determine what was really bothering Lauren. Lauren agreed to do this, and they made an appointment for the next day. She and Brad had talked, and she had asked that they not move forward with the wedding plans until she was sure getting married was the right thing to do. She said that she had no idea that Brad felt this way about how children should be raised, but she saw it as a very serious issue. Brad was not certain what made it such a serious issue, as he could also see that there were other alternatives such as hiring a live-in nanny. But he did agree with Lauren to put the wedding plans on hold until she was comfortable.

Lauren arrived for her counseling session the next day and found herself quite agitated about the meeting. She had planned what she wanted to say and had formulated some strong statements for the minister about the "proper place for women". She was ready to take him on and argue with him about his positions about women being in the home. As the minister started to speak, she became very aggressive and accused him of being very biased in his approach. The minister assured her again that he did not have a side on the issue. He said he had seen children raised successfully both by stay-at-home moms and by moms who worked. He inquired as to what Lauren thought about the intensity of her reaction.

Suddenly Lauren was in tears. She talked about having watched her father abuse her mother, both physically and emotionally as she grew up. She had vowed that she would never allow herself to be in a position in which she financially depended on a man. Lauren was convinced that if she had a good job in which she made a great deal of money that she would always be able to leave her husband if he ever was abusive to her. Lauren became aware that everything she had done in college had been designed to assure her that she could leave her husband if she needed to. She believed that had her mother had financial resources that her mother would have been able to protect herself from her husband.

Lauren had no evidence that Brad was in any way abusive to her. Brad had always expressed great concern for her and had always been very supportive of her desire to achieve. All the evidence she had was contrary to her need to protect herself, but her need for protection was not about her and Brad. She had simply learned that she would do the opposite of what her mother did, and she would, therefore, be safe in her marriage. Lauren was stunned that this had influenced so many of her life decisions. Lauren spent the next few months in therapy trying to find a more effective strategy to make sure she was protected in a marriage.

Lauren talked with Brad at length about her fears. She talked openly about her fears being based on what she had observed with her parents and the conclusions she had drawn about how women needed to protect themselves. Lauren was aware that this sense in her was strong and was unlikely to just go away. What she learned from therapy was that she could recognize the situation based on the facts, reason about how the situation could be handled from many different angles, and then with her husband make decisions about the well-being of their family that did not push her into a reactive position. Suddenly, Lauren saw many different options.

She and Brad explored several different strategies for having children and being responsible parents. Brad understood the situation and was very supportive of Lauren's need to know that she was protected should something go wrong with their marriage. He could see the wisdom of Lauren continuing to work when they had children in order to help her to manage the degree of threat she sensed about being a stay-at-home mom. Eventually after thinking the situation through very carefully, Brad and Lauren decided that Brad would make the best stay-at-home parent. He was excited about the prospect of being very involved in the rearing of their children, and she was secure that she could earn as good an income as Brad if not better.

We can see that emotional process that is learned through observing our families and not observing the availability of options can lead us to making life decisions that can impact the viability of our relationships as adults. It is important that we know about this type of learning and manage our reactivity through research, reason, and reflection. Had Lauren and Brad not gone through this process and worked on this issue prior to marriage, one day they would have faced the issue most likely without the benefit of counseling. Marriages can be severely stressed by these types of issues. If we have no way to understand the issues that trouble our marriages except through the understanding that we already have, we may damage our relationships beyond repair without meaning to do so.

What we are learning from our families is what poses a threat and how to respond to the threat when we see it. The learning is not so simple as our parents sit down and give us formulas to live life. All of this process happens without much awareness. At times, we can be dumbfounded as parents as to the decisions our children make in their intimate relationships. We wonder where in the world our children got their idea from, and yet, if we can step back from the situation, we can oftentimes see that we have imparted "wisdom" to our children based on how we managed challenges in our lives.

Lauren and Brad were fortunate. They learned from this situation that they could talk to one another and could find solutions based on collecting the facts, reasoning about how all the facts fit together, and then make a decision that is in the best interest of their family without hurting a family member. With research, reason, and reflection, we can solve problems in a manner that actually adds stability to a relationship. Problems are not problems. They are merely situations for which many solutions exist. This approach is far different than what most of us do today. Do you think that approaching life situations from this perspective makes good sense?

If it makes good sense to us, how do we think that we could learn this new strategy? Luckily we have all the necessary equipment to learn new strategies. Nature has provided us with a complete brain, and knowledge can be our guide as we learn something new. With accurate knowledge, we can negotiate intimate relationships with novel ideas that can bring us closer together and also allow us to become more mature Selves. Learning means that we must first pause to always ask our Selves if our understanding of the situation represents the facts. In Lauren's case, the facts were contrary to her fears. Secondly, we must ask how exactly it is that we are threatened. In some circumstances, we must ask exactly how it is we are safe. We can misperceive safety just like we can misperceive threat. Then we must ask our Selves how we learned the view that we currently hold. When we can access information to help us understand the root of our fear, we can deal with that fear in the appropriate context. In other words, when fears do not belong in our marriages, it is better if we reconcile the fears where they belong. Asking a marriage to resolve a past family issue is asking for failure. Our spouses cannot reconcile for us the hurts or threats we faced with our families. When we ask our marriages to reconcile our pasts for us, we place our marriages in harm's way. Anytime we place issues in a

84

marriage for resolution when the issue is illogical to the context of our marriage, we simply cannot come to a conclusion that does not end up hurting one party.

Had Lauren just gone along with her husband, she would have become reactive to multiple situations. Her reactivity would have led to destructive arguments, avoidances, pretends that everything was fine, or possibly her becoming very withdrawn and depressed. Our "symptoms" are connected to our emotional reactions. To correct this, we must have followed all the steps above, and then we must practice new behaviors based on a new way of seeing our Selves and our partners.

As we learned from the traffic light, we must practice for quite awhile before a new behavior becomes automatic. It will take failure as well as success to learn a new behavior. Failure can happen when we become increasingly threatened: we will lose our ability to engage in a logical train of thought. We must remember at these times that emotional reactions are natural responses to our situation; however, after we forgive our Selves as well as our spouses for an emotional response, we are responsible to do what we can to pull our Selves back to research, reason, and reflection as our formula to successful strategies to deal with life challenges. Anytime we are in the process of learning, we will find at times that we cannot access what we have just learned. The new learning, however, has not evaporated to be lost forever. Once we can re-engage in thought, we can once again use the new strategies we are learning. Eventually, the new strategies will seem "natural" to us, because these strategies are as much a part of our nature as are our emotions. This is critical to remember: all our adaptive strategies are part of our natures. We simply need to learn how to use which strategy under which circumstance. It can be learned, but knowing what we have learned is our only way to know what we need to correct.

Another example may help us to this more clearly. A young woman who marries a man who manages his threats about being intimate with another human being by over working finds herself alone many evenings far into the night. She may make advances to her husband and encourage him to be close to her. As he works more, her sense of threat increases, and she "pressures" him more to be close. He senses heightened threat, and uses the solution of distance that he has used for his lifetime. He works more, becomes less available, avoids the sense he has of himself as inept and unable to please his wife.

At work, no one questions his worth or his abilities; no one pushes him beyond his comfort level. He knows what to do at work and can be successful. At home, however, he senses himself in a very opposite way. Not knowing what to do with the situation at home promotes in this man a sense of threat about himself and about the relationship. If this man has handled most of life's difficulties by avoiding them and redirecting his energies to areas that are "safe", he will repeat the formula as he attempts to deal with his marriage. Working "solves" *his* problems in this marriage, but he forgets that another person's issues need to be addressed.

Suddenly he finds himself confronted with the fact that his wife is having an affair with her boss. He is forced to abandon the safety net of work and turn his attention to the threat he senses about being abandoned by his wife. As he focuses on her "inappropriate" behavior, he blames her for damaging the relationship. He is no longer, at least in his head, solely to blame for the outcome of the relationship. He has the evidence he needs to reinforce that relationships are risky business and that one should be careful about the level of involvement in them. At the same time, he wants this relationship with his wife. He loves her and wants to be meaningfully attached to her. He senses not being "safe" without her. The husband must now respond to a new sense of threat, but this time he fights.

The arguments are circular. His wife blames him for deserting her and leaving her vulnerable to another relationship, and he blames her for her lack of commitment to him. Bitter and desperate words increase the bitterness and hurt between them, and the desperation increases. From either of these positions, the relationship is on a fast, one-way track. Each has responsibility in the relationship being in its current state. Neither person knows what to do.

If he looks at his past as the "powerful force" that it is, he finds that he grew up with a mother who reacted to requests for intimacy by busying herself in "intellectual" pursuits. She cushioned the "demands" of her family on her by pursuing a career. When she was at home, she maintained a reserved, in control stance with her family and dealt with issues on an intellectual level. She was the voice of "reason". His mother taught him that threats could be managed by avoiding them through distraction. One could pretend to be calm by creating situations in which feelings were set aside. When one busies one's self with activity, life can appear free from anxiety, free from threat. The more one is not calm, the busier one must become. If a feeling distracts one, one can focus on what needs to be done and still appear as if everything is fine. In other words, the reaction to the sense of threat is to pretend that no threat is really there.

Feelings, in this family, were seen as "inferior" responses and not as reliable guides. His mother may indeed have had some wisdom, but ignoring feelings and not experiencing them is just another form of an emotional reaction. The bottom line is a feeling that may hurt you must be avoided: it must be responded to as if it is a threat. The markers for this family that a person is safe are that the person is highly productive in their work, that issues that are brought up are handled in an "intellectual" way (suggesting to a person to take a class at night if they miss their husband who is working late) coming up with a sensible solution, and that no one uses feelings to determine behavior. All life direction is determined by emotions, but this family promotes the belief that the direction of the family is derived from logic.

When the man's wife tells him about the affair giving him an alert that she needs to be intimate with him, he comes out fighting and is enraged that she has hurt him. She reacts to his response to her push for intimacy by becoming more threatened. She turns to her lover, thus widening the gap between them. She cannot understand her husband's response, because she does not see how he is threatened and does not see how he reacts to what is inside him. The response that he has given her when he works more tells *her* that he does not care about her, and yet, the response he has is his formula to *fix it for her*. These reactions are all each of them knows. Each person is caught intensely in their own interpretation of what is going on to the point that they cannot focus on what is happening for the other person.

Distraught, the young man turns to his mother. His wife is leaving him, and he finds himself alone. His mother gives him a "rational" explanation for what has happened in his relationship, and although she tells him that his reaction of being distraught is "normal", her own inability to be there for him pushes him deeper into a reaction. Her relationship with him is not calming, because her relationship is guided by the threat she senses when she is asked to be close: to be "real". She has taught him to not look to relationships for comfort, and she further reinforces this in him by the distance she maintains through an intellectual approach with her son about his "problem".

The mother seems as if she is connected. After all, she listened to her son: she has collected the "facts". She can relate to others what happened to her son in detail. She has heard the facts of his relationship: her marker that she is in touch with her son. The sense of threat, however, bubbles up in her each time she sees her son cry and bemoan his situation. This mother must do something to deny that something is amiss in her. She must quell her own anxiety, which means she must dispel his.

Instead of addressing her own discomfort and what issues about her own inadequacies his reaction brings up in her, she gives him advise based on the "facts". The situation is the same one the son created with his wife that led to his wife's affair. He is using the formulas his family has given him. His mother sees his reactivity as problematic instead of seeing his reactivity as the product of a problem. She cannot deal with the fact that her own distance impedes her son from having a close, intimate relationship with his wife that would keep his wife happy and safe within the confines of her marriage.

The mother coming to her son's aide will most likely reinforce in him the faulty formulas his mother has taught him. He senses a desperate need for the support at that moment, but unless he or his mother recognizes the reaction in his solutions to his marital problems, the son will probably not correct these dead end solutions. In-laws *are* part and parcel of our marital experiences. No one is to blame: it just happens, but it does not have to just happen.

His mother interprets his "need" for the relationship as a threat to him. His mother appears as if she *needs* no one and is *consistently in control* of her life. Although she says she understands, she comments on his reactivity to his dilemma in a way that indicates to him that he should be in better control of himself. Pretending to have knowledge and direction that one does not really have can calm a person but leave a system without direction. The mother had many "logical" formulas for handling problems, but she had failed to teach her son any formula for having a close and intimate relationship. The young man went to his mother for "help" and left believing something was wrong with him for not being able to be in control of him self. Without any help to see the facts of the situation, he will continue this pattern of reaction. His mother will reinforce his return to "productivity" and use this productivity as evidence that her son is "ok".

Her son is not ok, but to help him, she would have to question her own "protective" behaviors for managing her own sense of threat when asked to be "close". A mother who has been lucky enough to not have many stressors in her life can appear to be functioning well only to find as she watches her children flounder with life problems that she has taught them faulty formulas for having an intimate relationship. A fairly high percentage of mothers will not see their connections to their children's struggles with intimacy. It is those mothers who will be unable to "really" help their child as they grapple to be close. Fathers are in the same position. We teach only what we know. Our pasts do impact our marriages.

As the young man returns to being "productive" and busy with work, he will begin to sense a degree of calm that will reinforce the formula he uses to negotiate relationships. He will gain a false sense of being ok. He can see his mother as a wise woman who gave him helpful guidance. After all, he is calmer and is back to being productive. His formula, learned from his mother, will not be threatened again until the next relationship ends, but this time, the losing himself in his work may take longer to be as effective as it has been in the past. He may also have to do a lot more work (more hours and more crisis to resolve) to get the same payoff. His workplace will need to be demanding and chaotic to meet these requirements. Work places are more affected by our intimate relationships than we know. What can be a well-run organization can become a troubled work place when intimate relationships are disturbed.

The likelihood of him seeing the connection between his mother's sense of threat with intimacy and his own relationship struggles and eventually the problems that the office has is minimal without some help from outside his family system. Were his wife not so threatened by being "alone", she might be able to communicate to him in a way that would support his exploration of his reaction to the relationship. She, however, is as caught in an emotionally driven need as is her husband. Her family will probably provide her the same degree of "insight" into her dilemma as her husband's family provided him. Each family will "take sides" pointing out the "dysfunction" of the other and help their child to "move on" with his/her life. The couple will divorce, leaving the relationship with minimal learning about self in the context of intimacy. The next "life" lessons will be painful ones.

The alternative is for the husband to begin to question the formulas that he is using with his wife. If he could tell her that he recognizes that something is "wrong" and that he is willing to take a better look, she might be able to sit still long enough for someone to help him with his challenges. If she is willing to work to understand herself better, then the couple has a better chance at making their relationship work. Each must, however, focus on the definition of their own individual sense of threat, feelings that reinforce the sense of threat, learn how to use thought to help them assess whether or not the threat is real (who taught you this, how do they *know*, etc.), and finally work to define their own values, beliefs, and principles from which they can actually live their lives.

The process to define one's self and to learn to function maturely in an intimate relationship takes as long as it takes to divorce, meet someone else, and find one's self right back in the same position. The life energy will take about the same. The hurt and anxiety involved will be equal as well. The financial devastation will not be the same. The outcome, however, for working on Self as well as the relationship is that one has a spouse who is really present: the relationship is alive—each person senses fully the passion, the comfort, the joy, and the connection. Children can continue to be raised by two parents who can relate openly to one another. In-laws can have family gatherings on holidays, and children learn to react and to feel with thought as their guide. The reward is major, and the legacy is that the formula is passed along to our off-spring. *The cycle*

of divorce can stop, but <u>BOTH</u> people must engage in facing the fears that keep us acting like animals on the African plains.

All life form's first sense of any stimulus is to assess for threat/non-threat. That is the emotional system that is based on instinct. It is important to assess for threat, but we fail to assess based on more than just the sense of threat. When a predator is about to bite your butt, instant reactions can be advantageous. When your partner is asking you to be close, instant reactions most likely will not be helpful.

We must become more curious creatures if we are to come to know each other. We must become aware of our emotional reactions, assess our feelings and the sense of threat, and then behave based on what we think is best for our Selves and for others who we say are important to us. It is thought that can help to become calm. We can define our values, our beliefs, and our principles, and from those behave in ways that genuinely express the caring and commitment we have for others. When we are committed, which comes from using research, reason, and reflection to define our Selves, we have built in guidance systems that override the fear generated from sensing threat. We know we will behave honorably and that others who are close to us will do the same. Our brains help us to know the difference between those who are reacting to life circumstances and those who mean us harm. We can operate from reality. When we experience those who mean us harm, then we can mobilize our behavior around the parameters of our values and beliefs and protect our Selves based on a real need to do so. Then we can be like the creatures on Galapagos.

END OF CHAPTER WORK

We are all in situations that result in us not being as close to our intimate other as we would like. We can use the exercise below to help us think about our reactivity and the reactivity of our mate. The exercise will help us think of strategies to help us know our own sense of threat better, which can help us to manage our reactivity and feelings. Remember, decisions made when we are CALM offer us the best opportunity to make decisions that can promote wisdom in our life choices.

What were the most important thoughts we had as we read this chapter?

What makes these thoughts important to us?

How can we describe what we think we may have learned from our families about our reactions in our marriages?

Are our reactions to our spouse sensible in terms of the facts and how the facts fit together?

Are our reactions promoting the well-being of our families as well as of our Selves?

What would have to be different between us and our spouse to be like the creatures who live on Galapagos?

What would be different for us on a day-to-day basis if we were like the creatures on Galapagos?

These descriptions illustrate how emotional reactivity promotes patterns that harm marital relationships. We have all taken steps like and experienced deep disappointment and hurt. We also can take steps that are thoughtful, but in order to do so, we must actually be able to think. Compare the two distinct ways of perceiving and interpreting situations. Which do you believe is in the best interest of the relationship? What would need to be different for you to be able to use thought to help you with your relationship challenges?

THE DIFFERENCE BETWEEN REACTING AND THINKING ABOUT RELATIONSHIP CHALLENGES	
EMOTIONALLY REACTIVE DECISION MAKING	**THOUGHTFUL DECISION MAKING**
Wife: Senses being very lonely and uncertain of herself while her husband is at work.	Wife: Begins to explore the source of her discomfort when she is along. Can manage the discomfort with objective assessment and greater understanding of herself as a product of her parent's relationship.
Wife: Attempts to seduce her husband to get him to come from work early one evening when he calls to let her know he will be late again.	Wife: Reports to her husband that she finds herself lonely without him and would like for them to find a way to spend more time together.
Husband: Hears his wife as telling him that he is not being a very good husband. He does not know what to do to fix the problem: he	Husband: Hears his wife's dilemma and understands that her dilemma is connected to him in some way. Tells her that although

senses that he is not "good" enough for her and will not be able to meet her needs. As he hangs up the phone, he realizes that he has disappointed her by not coming home from work and begins to worry about being an inadequate husband.	~~he cannot come home~~ immediately, he will take some time the following afternoon for them to be together and talk through what is bothering her. He recognizes that he has a tendency to be distant from others and is willing to explore the possibility that his distance through work is impacting the marriage negatively.
Husband: Returns to the task at hand at work. His boss comes in to chat for a few minutes, reviews his work, and tells him that is a very valued employee who will climb the corporate ladder very quickly with the long hours he is putting into his job. His sense of self is bolstered. Here at his job, he knows exactly what is expected of him and how to do what is expected. He enjoys the rewards that he earns. He gets lost in his work, looks up several hours later to realize the he has worked far beyond the time he intended to work. On the drive home, he begins to "prepare" himself to face an angry wife. He decides that his best defense will be an offense and begins to explore ways he can excuse himself from responsibility and make his wife responsible for the "problem"	Husband: Realizes that he has worked far later than he meant to and recognizes that neglecting his wife is a signal that he is using distance from her to manage the discomfort of being close. He begins to ask himself questions about how he can understand his discomfort based on what he knows about how his mother and father related to one another. On the way home, he thinks about discussing this with his wife and providing her extra emotional support when he gets home, even though she may be very angry with him.
Husband: Walks in the door and realizes that his wife is still awake.	Husband: Comes in the door and immediately goes to the bedroom

He pretends not to notice hoping to avoid her and stops by the kitchen. He gets a beer and pops the top slipping quietly into the side den closing the door gently behind him. His wife gets up thinking that she heard a noise and finds him in the den. He tells her that he did not want to wake her and that he had to work later than he thought. He relates what the boss said hoping it will make her less angry. She says she wishes she were as important to him as his work. He says, "What the hell does that mean? Who do you think I am doing this for anyway? What do you expect? Did you think I wouldn't have to freakin' work or something? How do you think you get all the things you want?" All of his rehearsal on the way home pays off. He was ready for her.

to let his wife know that he regrets he has been remiss in watching the time and thus in attending to her needs. He asks her if she would like to have a beverage from the kitchen. When she says, "Why would you bother with me now--- you haven't been all evening?", he responds with, "I deserve that. I am willing to talk about this. I was thinking on the way home that I am avoiding something with you. I want to get to the bottom of this."

Wife: Is very upset that her husband will not see her point. She goes to bed very angry with him that he is so selfish and self-centered. She sees herself as inconsequential to him. The next morning when she arrives at work, her boss says something to her about her seeming upset. She tells her boss that she and her husband had a few words the night before and that she did not sleep very well. Her boss touches her on the

Wife: Is very upset with her husband and has lots of trouble sleeping. She takes a few minutes the next morning before beginning work to take a walk. She attempts to understand the chain of events. From work, she calls her husband to tell him that she would like some time to talk but plans to write him a letter just in case something happens that they cannot talk about this. She works on what the pattern is that is arm and says that he is sorry and that if she needs a shoulder to cry on, he is there for her. That afternoon, as she is working, she becomes aware that she is "looking" for him. She remembers how he touched her arm. Late in the afternoon, her husband calls to let her know he will be late again. Even though he says he is sorry, she feels that once again, he is putting their relationship on the backburner. She is upset to think that she will be spending another evening alone. As she gets off the phone, her boss passes by and asks how she is doing. She says she is pissed. Her husband has to work again. The boss suggests they have a drink and let her get it out of her system. Even though she sense that the situation may not be something that is a good idea, she also senses some relief in believing that someone really cares how she is feeling.

developing between them. She tells her husband in her letter to him that she wants to understand both their parts in the relationship. She sees the "problem" clearly as simply a matter of on-going work to make the relationship stronger. She calls a friend for lunch, not to bash her husband but to get some emotional support. Her husband is relieved that his wife seems understanding and supportive and will be able to talk with him without blaming him for the problem or telling him that he is inadequate. When the wife's boss comments on if she is okay, she responds that she is having a minor personal problem but is fine.

Husband: Takes off a few minutes early to try to get his wife off his back. When he arrives at home, no one is there. His wife comes home fairly late, and he becomes very angry with her that she went out to dinner with her boss. He senses a high degree of threat inside himself and instead of expressing his emotions and feelings to his wife,	Husband: Gets off early from work to go home to talk to his wife. He realizes that she is not home. Although he sense some panic in himself about where his wife is, he talks to her about what it was really like for him to come home and realize that she was not there. He talks about his absence and how that must have impacted

he yells at her about having been out when they could have been spending time together. He covers up his deep concern with anger that promotes a misperception on her part that he does not really care about her. They have another argument, and tonight they sleep in separate rooms.	her decision to go out. When she tells him that she was with her boss, he again senses some panic but takes responsibility for having not provided appropriate emotional support for her. He is aware of his reactions and deals openly about his reactions with his wife. She senses that he is connected to her and wants to be of support.
Wife: The next morning at work, she is aware that she is looking for her boss----more aware of his presence that she has been in the past. She smells his cologne as he passes her. He reaches over her desk to discreetly ask how things are at home. She blushes as she has a feeling for him that she has not had before. Her husband calls on the phone and she does not report to him that her boss is standing at her desk. When her husband says he loves her, she does not respond, because she does not want her boss to no longer be interested in her. Her husband senses threat that he told her he loved her, and she did not respond. Inside himself, he wonders what she ever saw in him anyway.	

CHAPTER FIVE

BASIC FACT # 3
People need relationships with each other and also need to be individual selves.

On planet earth deep in summer in the foothills of the mountains of East Tennessee, one can gaze upon a spectacular light show. Fireflies fill the night sky blinking their presence in hopes of soliciting a relationship. They urge the other, "PICK ME, PICK ME " by using patterned flashes of light that tell the other "I AM THE ONE". The female, who stays on the ground, flashes back a light pattern to the male in flight. Her hope is to either capture a mate or to dine. If it is a mate she desires, and the male responds, both forge a relationship in which off-spring is the outcome. If it is dinner she desires, and the male responds, both establish a prey/predator relationship in which the male loses his life. The outcome is vastly different. Relating can be treacherous business.

In the same small town, human beings engage in behaviors in bars that say "PICK ME, PICK ME". These human beings use patterned behaviors recognized by one another as telling the other "I AM THE ONE". The general hope is to catch a mate or to find someone who can help squelch the sense of loneliness that threatens the sense of whom we are, preferably without becoming someone's dinner. If it is a mate we desire and the other person responds in kind, we marry and plan to build a life together. We see our Selves as enriched, as being acceptable, and lovable. Whether or not the marriage is built on a solid commitment will not be an issue until later in the relationship. For the moment, just having someone who "wants to *be* with us" gives us what we need.

If we desire only to squelch the anxiety building up in us about being alone, to feed our emaciated sense of Self, without possessing the skills to negotiate the soon to come sense of losing Self in the relationship, then one of us will sense having been someone's dinner. We need the connection, and yet, our fears about connections will result in a one-night stand. We see our Selves as having been used, as having been exploited. We walk away from the relationship sensing being less than we were when we encountered the person in the bar. Our anger about being used may bolster a false sense of Self, long enough for us to find our next "relationship".

We behave these ways and fail to see how we are like the tiny beetles that have the incredible ability to "light up" and take to field and wood to live out their lives. Our lives are not as simple as fireflies', but we also do not have the simple brain system of a firefly. We have the ability to pull back and reflect on our behavior in relationships. We have the ability to think, reason, and reflect, but our tendency is to react. We have choice, but we do not choose. Our feelings and our ancient sense of threat are strong forces to prevent thought. When we cannot think about our lives and how we, like other life forms, behave obeying simple, rudimentary laws of nature, then we are bound to not having an understanding of our Selves that can help us to behave differently.

In order to not engage in simplistic emotional behaviors that are like other beings, we must come to understand how the forces of Nature and Nurture influence our need to be a distinct and separate Self that we defend when we sense that we are threatened. We must also understand how the forces of Nature and Nurture influence our need to be connected to others as a method of defense for our Selves when we are threatened. It is our emotional responses that shift us back and forth in our struggles to stay safe in a relationship, and both instinct and learning have equal impact on how these struggles affect our relationships.

NATURE

Nature provides us every adaptive strategy that we need to stay safe. We use these adaptive strategies to perceive and interpret the environment and then to behave. Each of our perceptual systems is necessary for our safety. Each system offers us different adaptive advantages, and it is up to us to know which one to use for specific situations. Misused an adaptive advantage may not provide us protection but may place us in harm's way. Unless we can distinguish when to use which adaptive advantage, we may find our Selves very symptomatic. The process of learning begins at birth, and we hope to have mastery of these adaptive strategies by the time we leave the protection of our parents. Many variables can influence the success of our learning. The primary function of parents is to teach us how to keep our Selves safe. But, it is nature that sets up the dilemma for us to figure out.

Having three distinct systems from which to perceive and interpret our environments has advantages in and of itself. In the middle of a crisis, it is not to our advantages to have to stop and think through a situation to determine if we are in danger or not. We need instant, automatic behavior available to us. We have that. Our perceptual systems scan every input into our system to assess for our safety. When an input is deemed "unsafe", we automatically react to protect our Selves. If an input is deemed safe, then we are free to access other behaviors based on the other two perceptual systems. Having all three systems functional is truly to our advantage. The emotional system is the building block upon which all life depends. The subjective system is available to some forms of life. The objective system is available to fewer forms of life. We are in the last category. We can see that we have more adaptive strategies available to us than any other life form, and yet, we find our Selves in major dilemmas about relationships. How can we have more adaptive strategies than any other life form and be messing up our relationships the way we are?

Part of the answer lies in the basic dilemma we face as infants. As an infant, we have two basic needs that we must meet if we are to survive. When survival is on the line, our behaviors are all based on our emotions. The world is simple: I have a need, it is life threatening if it is not met, I behave in a way to elicit someone to take care of me, my need is met, and I am calm. When I am calm, I am free to rest, to interact with my environment with the few skills I have, and have my needs met. When I do not have my needs met, I sense threat and behave accordingly. Babies have the same strategies that we have for responding to threat, but the strategies are less sophisticated than those of an adult (if everything has gone well as we grow toward maturity). Once a baby senses threat and is reacting based on instinct, the relationship system may be threatened, and yet, that is the very essence of life as an infant. So, a baby is in a dilemma at birth. It must function as an independent Self physiologically, but-----and this is a huge but----- it must also form a relationship with a caregiver to insure its survival. When the relationship is formed with a caregiver who has an accurate perception of need, the infant is safe. Relationships are experienced as safe. The baby then can engage in other behaviors that further the connection in the relationship. When the relationship is not formed with the caregiver or the caregiver does not have an accurate perception of the baby's needs, the baby experiences the relationship as not safe. The implications follow us all the way into adulthood and into our marriages.

What happens to us as infants is genuinely quite important. As much as we would like to believe when things go wrong that parents are not responsible, parents are indeed responsible to help us to balance our need to be a Self and our need for a relationship. Our early years are critical ones. If we did not get what we needed from our parents, blaming them will not help. We must realize that this is a MULTIGENERATIONAL process: responsibility is not solely on the shoulders of our parents. Circumstances also impact the ability of our parents to function at any given point in time. If our parents are experiencing a threat from their environment, then our parents may not be able to respond to us in the most helpful way to increase our potential to learn about being a Self and about being in a relationship with another person. This explains the individual differences that we see in the outcome of raising children. We apply the same methods, and yet, some children find life as an adult easier than other children do. As a parent, if we are experiencing threatening situations our behaviors are limited. Our access to research, reason, and reflection is restricted, and we may not be as helpful in our responses. Many life circumstances impact how we perform as parents to help our children.

As parents we face dilemmas. We rarely receive feedback from anyone who can assist us with parenting. It is a delicate subject to approach. For a good number of us, we experience any feedback that could be perceived or interpreted as critical as a threat. We react accordingly which may result in the loss of the feedback. A person who is trying to help us to be a better parent may be seen as a threat. If we react in a way that poses a threat to the person who was giving us feedback, we stand a good chance of not having any additional feedback. The job of being a parent is one of the most important that we will ever take on in our lives, and yet, there is no one to do an objective evaluation for us. In any other job, we would consider this ridiculous. We train for being a parent at the knees of our own parents. Whatever limits our parents have will become our own limits. We can move beyond these boundaries, but if we are able to do so, it is because we research, reason, and reflect. The early years are sensitive for us as parents and for us as children. The dilemma imposes constraints on our functioning at a time when it is important to be at our best.

Situations can enhance our being at our best. When we look at other social systems with other animals we see a great deal of involvement of the rearing of young by many adults. We may say, well, we have teachers and school systems to help us to raise our children, but teachers are not free to set limits with our children, and they must be very cautious about the feedback they give us as adults. Ask any professional person who must give feedback to parents about the job they are doing as parents, and they will tell you, it is tricky business. When a parent recognizes that some thing is not going well with their child, and the parent wants to know what they may be doing that is not helpful, then a parent may receive feedback and use it to research, reason, and reflect. Grandparents face the dilemma of very possibly being heard as being critical of their child or of the child's spouse. The other side of the situation is that far too often people become critical of a parent instead of stepping back to try to understand what challenges the parent may be facing that interferes with their success. When these questions are not posed, interventions will fall short of their mark. What children learn when parents experience a situation as threatening is to react to feedback or other stressors that present themselves. Learning to react to feedback or stress limits our capacity to respond to our environments.

The act of researching, reasoning and reflecting teaches a child that these are effective strategies. This is true when we are giving feedback to our children as well. Feedback that is open and non-judgmental helps a child to gain a clearer sense of self. Telling a child point blank that his or her project is not very good and giving him or her specific examples where improvements could be made is far different than telling a child that an average project is excellent. A child depends of us as parents for reliable feedback. Screaming at a child that they could never do any thing right is also not helpful. Neither seeing a child's work as always excellent or telling a child they never do any thing right cannot be an accurate point of view. Any parent who uses either of these strategies is a parent who sees the world from a threatened perspective. For a parent to give a child realistic feedback, the parent must not see the child as needing protection, *and the parent must not be assessing his or her own worth through the accomplishments of the child.* Reliable feedback encourages competence in children. The more competent sense of Self that is developed by a child, the more the child can use relationships as resources. The very act of protecting a child when the child does not need protection lowers the probability that a child will develop a competent sense of Self. The very act of not protecting a child when a child needs protection lowers the probability that a child will develop a competent sense of self. Without this competence, a child does not grow up with a sense of safety about relationships.

What we are seeing as we are describing this process of raising children is that nature and nurture is interwoven tightly and determines how well we function. Understanding that we are predisposed to behave certain ways and understanding that it is learning that helps us to select from the adaptive strategies available to us is critical to our being able to make a difference for our Selves. Learning does not end at eighteen: we are learners for all of our lives. Corrections can be made, but we must know what is available to us before we can make corrections. We must take steps to research, reason, and reflect if we are to make a difference in our own lives.

RESEARCH: To research, we must be open to discovering that we have an erroneous view of certain things. Research means that we gather facts. If we believe that we already know the facts, we will not search for the facts. All too often in our intimate relationships we believe we know what is happening, when we are actually in the dark. If we marry as virtual strangers in an attempt to secure a relationship, we cannot possibly know the other person. And, if we do not know our Selves, then we cannot reveal who we are.

It is factual that we cannot begin to fully research, reason, and reflect until our late teens. Given that we do not have full capacity to think available to us until our late teens, it would be unrealistic to expect that we would know our Selves in our early adult years. Knowing our Selves matters when we begin to have intimate relationships. We lack the awareness that we do not know our Selves, so it is unlikely that any of us will work on the project of defining a Self. For the most part, we adopt the strategies of our parents or assume that doing the opposite of our parents will work in our intimate relationships. Without collecting facts, we are caught in the "facts" of others. That leaves us being less than a Self. When we are less than a Self, we are more apt to find our Selves threatened in some way by our relationships. If we were to pause to describe our Selves to a stranger, what would we say? How do we get to the facts about who we are?

If we accept the premise that our parents are our teachers, then to begin to discover the facts about who we are, we need to discover the facts about who our parents are. We must come to know our histories. When we see any wise leader of a nation or a group, that person knows the facts about how the nation or organization came to be. This person would use the facts from the past to help guide current and future decisions. It is the same with our lives. We fail, far too often, to behave as if our lives are important and deserve time to plan and to think. We act as if we can just go out and live life in a complex world without thinking about it, and everything will be okay. The complexities we face today demands thought. Without thought, we are plain lucky if our lives turn out okay. At a time when we generally turn away from our parents or collapse into our parents' lives, defining our Selves provides us an effective strategy to enhance the likelihood that our lives will be what we want them to be.

Coming to know our families, who each person is and how they view the world, is a helpful way to gather information. This information is what we use to help us to define who we are. Once we have formed a solid definition of our Selves, we can negotiate a relationship without our relationships posing threats to us. Self is essential to a calm, productive relationship in which all members of the relationship can experience safety. Part of being safe means that the partners in a relationship are not constantly caught in the struggle to either make sure the relationship is okay or to try to get out of the relationship. In other words, the sense of threat is minimal, and when a sense of threat exists, the partners talk openly and seek solutions. In such an environment, people thrive, reaching full potentials while also aiding others in their quests for life dreams.

Collecting information from family members means just that. The objective is to collect the information. The objective is not to heal old wounds, try to place blame, or form a relationship that has been non-existent. If healing is a side outcome or developing a meaningful connection is a side outcome, that is a plus. Seeking to heal a relationship or trying to form a meaningful connection is merely the product of needing to seek safety: it is part of an emotional process and will not be productive. The questions that elicit information have to do what happened when, who did what then, and what do you think about what happened. When we begin to hear life stories, we will have a great deal of information to help us piece together who we really are. The stories we hear will most likely not be objective. The stories are merely each person's version of what happened. Some facts are part of these stories but some parts of the stories will be filled with the distortions that our own minds create. We must recall that our perceptions and interpretations are highly susceptible to error. If we hear enough life stories from many different family members----our parents, our aunts and uncles, our grandparents and our great aunts and great uncles----then we can eventually get some idea about what most likely happened.

REASON: To reason means to gain understanding about the patterns that have formed in our families and helped to shape who we are. It is a way to put the pieces together. We can make sense of life events when we are able to reason. Reason requires having objective facts. We know that many of the "facts" we collect must be assessed for objectivity. We all are prone to lose our objectivity when we experience an incident between our Selves and another person that results in the sense of threat. The important thing to do in these circumstances is not to debate or take sides, but listen, *and continue to ask questions.* Patterns will emerge as we hear these life stories, and suddenly things we did not understand before will make great sense to us.

We must sift through the stories we hear and try to understand the emotional response of each person involved. We must remember that an emotional response occurs when a person senses a threat in a relationship or fails to recognize a threat that actually exists. We will begin to see our Selves and our own tendency toward certain perceptions and interpretations of life situations. Some family members will be less threatened than others. Look at what each person does and how he or she handles life circumstances. What life decisions has each person made? How did they make these decisions? Are we following any patterns that our family established? It is easy to gather the information as we simply show a genuine interest in another person's life. With practice, it becomes easier to see how a person has reacted and how the reaction impacted the outcome of the situation. Ask people about life regrets. After we have gathered information and we understand how the information fits together to form patterns in our families' lives, we are ready to reflect on our Selves in the context of our families.

REFLECTION: To reflect means that we take into consideration all individuals in our relationship system, as well as our Selves. It is important to know how our families have considered each member of the family in major decision-making. We have three choices in response to our reflection on our Selves and our relationships.

We can become Selfish. When we are selfish and unaware of others or uncaring about others, we are reacting based on the emotional reaction to threat. We sense some need to protect our Selves based on this threat. Sensing threat means that we cannot research, reason, or reflect, and that means our behavior is very limited. With limited behavior, we react to our partners in ways that do not promote the health of the relationship. Our partners eventually will react to protect him or her Self. We can begin to see that our relationship will become much more complex based on a series of emotional reactions. The more intense the emotional reactions become, the less likely the couple will be to get the relationship back on track. Emotional reactions can become very destructive to a relationship. We can address this issue by gathering facts about the threat we experience, understanding how we came to sense threat, and then working to consider others. When we can become factual and objective, we can alter our behaviors.

We can also become Selfless. When we are selfless, we are either unaware of our own needs or unable to express our needs for fear that we may lose our relationship. We think that being selfless would be most harmful to our Selves, but being selfless places demands on the other person to be in charge of the relationship. When we place others in charge of the relationship, eventually we will experience the relationship as threatening, and our partner will experience his or her sense of Self as threatened. Again, we begin to see a circular pattern of emotional reactivity that is destructive to a relationship. Learning to be more of a Self, means that we will have to explore who we are, to understand that our sense of threat is unrealistic, and then begin to practice our new behaviors.

Being a Self means that we balance our need for a Self and our need for a relationship. Part of balancing these two needs is simply recognizing that both needs are natural and that we will shift back and forth between an awareness of each need. Sensing the need for more Self does not mean that we have to see the relationship as a threat. Sensing the need for more relationship does not mean that being a Self is a threat. It is possible for both people in a relationship to be aware of emotional process and openly talk about what is happening in the relationship. When we can be open with our partners, we do not have to be threatened. We can be secure in knowing that each of us is committed to the relationship: this is part of our defining our Selves. What our parents teach us will determine how much we experience threat when we sense needs for Self or relationships.

As we can see, objectivity offers us many more alternatives than our emotional system offers us. Objectivity gives us adaptive advantages in dealing with complex relationship systems. It is our only hope to have a strong sense of Self and an intimate, committed relationship. Both a strong sense of Self and an intimate and committed relationship provide us safety. From a sense of safety, we can be extremely productive human beings. Translating these ideas to every day behavior requires practice. An example may help us to see how research, reason, and reflection can help us to achieve a stronger definition of self.

Leslie had been experiencing problems in her relationships with men. She was in her early thirties and had divorced her first husband. After the divorce, she had been involved with several men. Each relationship began very intensely and then ended abruptly, usually after a serious argument. Leslie knew something was wrong. She could excuse the relationships ending, because she could identify the fault of the man she was seeing that led to her getting very angry. After awhile, however, Leslie began to think that more was happening than she was aware of.

Leslie decided to get some help to discover what she needed to do differently. The therapist Leslie saw had studied Bowen Family Systems Theory. To Leslie, she could care less about the orientation of her therapist. She just wanted help. She had wondered if she had some kind of a personality disorder or if she needed medications to help her control her anger. The therapist said he thought he could help her without giving her a diagnosis or without her taking some medications, but it would require that Leslie challenge some of her thinking about her Self and her relationships with other people. The therapist took a very good family history with Leslie. Leslie was surprised by how little she knew about her family.

As she discussed her family history with the therapist, she became aware that she had a very definite pattern in her relationships with men that somewhat mimicked her pattern of her relationships with her family. Her family had intense relationships with each other that every now and them erupted into highly conflicted episodes. People would stop speaking for a while and would talk to other members of the family about what happened. Eventually something would happen that would bring the two people back into contact with each other and the intense closeness would begin all over again. The major difference was that the conflicted episodes ended the relationships that Leslie had with men. Her therapist suggested that she might find it helpful to learn more about her family and what other patterns she might be repeating in her relationships. He also told her about the way her brain worked and how sensing threat could lead to automatic behavior that was not always helpful to relationships.

Some things the therapist said really clicked for Leslie. She could see how she lost herself at the beginning of a relationship wanting desperately to form some kind of meaningful attachment that would last. Without a relationship, Leslie sensed being alone and scared. She definitely could see how the threat of being alone was propelling her behavior. In order to get a guy interested in her, she engaged in several emotional reactions: pretend---acting interested in things that he talked about, acting as if she was not upset about something he did when she was hurt by it, and ignoring her own interests in favor of what he wanted to do. Leslie was afraid if she showed people who she really was they would not like her and would not have her be a part of their lives. Her solution was to pretend to be someone she was not. Leslie also noted that she had a definite pattern of sleeping with men early in her relationship with them. As she thought about this in the context of threat, she saw that she slept with them as a way to interest them in her.

Not too long into the relationship, Leslie began to sense that she was being taken for granted. She would become angry that they never did any of the things she enjoyed, she felt used sexually, she missed her friends and her family, and she found the man boring. She got tired of cooking him dinner all the time and of him bringing his laundry over for her to do. While it was true that Leslie had suggested she cook for him after he got off work, and she had suggested that she do his laundry with hers, she had also thought that he would offer to do something in return for her. When she hinted at him doing something and he had not responded, she sensed very threatened that he really did not care for her. Leslie was caught in a dilemma of wanting the man in her life but not wanting to give up her Self to have him there. Leslie went back and forth between trying to get a relationship going to trying to get out of a relationship. Eventually the man did just one more thing to disregard her, and Leslie let him have what he deserved. He too had his laundry list for her. The relationship ended as quickly as it began. Leslie immediately became depressed and started searching again for Mr. Right, because she sensed threat at the prospect of being alone.

At her next therapy session, she talked with her therapist about how she could see how experiencing threat was resulting in her being in and out of relationships. Leslie told her therapist that she thought one thing she might work on to reduce the threat would be to be more of a Self from the beginning of the relationship. The therapist wondered how she had learned to be threatened about being alone, which sparked some ideas for Leslie. The therapist suggested she sit down with the family history he had drawn out and see if trying to understand how she might have learned to sense threat would give her some more idea about how to do something different. The therapist suggested that talking to some of her family might help her to figure out what was happening with her in relationships.

Leslie planned a trip to her hometown for that weekend and just went home to visit her parents. As she spent time with them doing laundry and raking leaves, Leslie asked questions. She wondered with her mother how she managed to have been married and stayed married to her husband even though her husband had not been faithful to her mother. She wondered with her father what it had been like for him to settle down as a very young man when there was so much he had not experienced. In other words, Leslie just had conversation with her family that was directed at learning how they saw relationships and how they balanced out the need for a Self and the need for a relationship.

What Leslie heard was very helpful to her. Her mother told her that she had married fairly young. Her father had abandoned the family when she was very young, forcing her mother to go to work in a factory. When Leslie's mother was young, it was not proper for women to work. This separated Leslie from the rest of her schoolmates. She never felt like she was accepted and spent a great deal of time alone. She blamed her mother for her father abandoning them. She thought her mother could have done something to keep her husband from leaving them. Without a father, Leslie's mother's life was miserable. To Leslie's mother, the most important thing was having the security of a father in the house. Leslie asked if her mother had ever thought of leaving her husband, and her mother told her that she still thought of leaving him. When Leslie asked why she had never left, her mother told her that she was afraid that she could not support herself or her children when they were younger.

Leslie's father told her some interesting things as well. When he had met Leslie's mother he was a very young man. His father had died when he was very young, and his mother could not take care of his brothers and him. The children ended up moving from one family member's home to the other with brief periods with his mother. He never sensed that he had a family and was delighted when he met Leslie's mother. Her family had been very welcoming of him. He fit right in, and it was not long before he married Leslie's mother. Leslie

110

had always believed that he had hated her mother's family and was surprised to hear that he had been so eager to become a part of the family. He went on to tell Leslie that soon after the marriage, he felt a lot of pressure from his mother-in-law to take care of all the family. He saw his mother-in-law as very demanding and overly involved in his decision-making about his new family. Leslie asked her dad if he had ever considered a divorce. He responded with he had, but he knew how important it was to keep the family together.

Leslie went back to her next therapy session and reported about the information she had gathered. She was seeing how her family had shaped her own reactions based on threats they had experienced growing up. Leslie became more intrigued to learn about how much of her behavior with men had to do with what her family had taught her. It was like a whole new viewpoint was opening up for Leslie. Leslie suddenly began to see her Self as a natural outcome of the family in which she had been raised, in addition to seeing how she was using adaptive strategies in settings that did not make sense.

We can begin to see how Leslie was able to gather information, understand how the pieces of information fit together, and how people had given up a sense of Self based on threat. it made sense to her that she was so desperate for a relationship and saw her Self as incapable of being on her own. It also made sense to her that she would be hypersensitive to giving up her Self to get a relationship.

We know that working on being a Self takes time. It is hard work, but it is this type of discovery that can alter our worldview and allow us to make some changes in who we are. These changes can make it more possible for us to have an intimate relationship without sensing threat. We can form intimate, fulfilling relationships but only after we have worked to define our Selves. What do we have to do to define a Self? How does it work? Can we do this work and stay in our relationships? To answer these questions we need to turn toward understanding how learning influences how we define our Selves.

NURTURE

We know that our families teach us to discriminate between threat and safety. They are our learning ground. It is not that our parents sit down and tell us what is threatening and what is safe. We usually learn from experience with them and from observation. We do not have access to memories of our early experiences. But we can remember some things that happen to us early in our childhoods. Knowing about our experiences through memory to help us to gather information about what we have learned is difficult. We do, however, have a window into how our parents view what is threatening and what is safe.

As we work to begin to define a Self, one of the most important exercises we can do is to sit down and define our values, beliefs, and principles. Doing this can give us essential information that can give us a direction to start making real changes in our lives. The exercise is more demanding than we might think. Suddenly we can tell how solid a Self we have defined up this point in our lives. The exercise can also point out to us where we need to focus our life energy to achieve change. To do so, we need to understand what values, beliefs, and principles are.

A *value* is what we deem to be important to us. That sounds simple enough, but when we start to list our values, it becomes more difficult to define what these are. The most important factor we need to think about as we determine our values is to pose the question: how did I come to hold this value. What about his is important to me? For example, we may say that we value honesty. Honesty is the ability to be open with another human being about a situation. That sounds like an important value to have if we want to have a stable relationship with another human being. That is what makes the value important. That brings us to our beliefs. Our *beliefs* are what we accept as accurate. In the case of honesty, a belief may be that to have a stable relationship, we must be honest with each other. This sounds like a sound idea. Probably most people would agree with this belief. Next comes the way we define our principles. Our *principles* are the guidelines we use to determine our behaviors based on our values and our beliefs. We use our principles to tell us what to do under specific circumstances. In the instance of honesty, we would tell the truth about a situation to our partner.

This sounds like a simple enough formula to define a Self. So how do we explain that we can become so threatened about not having enough Self? Using the example above about honesty, we can discover what goes awry. If we say that we value honesty, and we say that we believe honesty is essential to a stable relationship, then what prompts us to lie to our partners on a regular basis? The answer is simple. We become concerned that if we tell the truth, we may lose the relationship, the other person may think less of us, we may argue with our spouse, we may not get what we want, and the list goes on. We justify the lie we tell. In other words, we sense a threat and abandon our values, beliefs, and principles to protect our Selves. It is automatic. Unless we recognize this inconsistency and discipline our Selves to research, reason, and reflect, we can anticipate that we will continue abandoning our values, beliefs, and principles. Once we abandon our values, beliefs, and principles, then we face a real threat to our sense of Self. It is up to us to define our Selves and live that definition. Using research, reason, and reflection we can become a more solid Self.

The formula of gathering information, understanding how the information fits together, and reflecting on how each person can be considered while also respecting our Selves helps us to define our Selves more solidly. In other words, we have struck the balance between being Selfish and Selfless. Again, we need to go back to our learning ground to get the information we need. Looking to our families to research, reason, and reflect, we gain amazing insight into what makes us tick. If we decide to redefine our values, beliefs, and principles, then we must be able to define what these currently are, understand the reasoning behind these, and redefine our values, beliefs, and principles based on reality. Our values, beliefs, and principles are learned from our families. We use their values, beliefs, and principles as if these are our own.

Most of us have never taken the time to define our values, beliefs, and principles. Trying to sit down and define these is a difficult task, and yet, if we had spent any time defining them, we would be able to easily list them. For each value, we can list a belief. For each value and belief, we can list a principle. What we find when we list our values, beliefs, and principles is that some of these are helpful and some of these are not helpful to us. For instance, if we say that we value having a relationship that is intimate. We go further to say that we believe we should make lasting commitments in our intimate relationships. We then take the last step and make the commitment to stay with our partner no matter what. In the event that we have a child to die and each of us experiences a difficult adjustment period, it is logical to stay with the relationship. In the event that our spouse beats us, it is illogical to stay in the relationship. Our values, beliefs, and principles are tied to our emotional system. Whether or not we are threatened determines how closely we can live our values, beliefs, and principles. We cannot live a principles life unless we use research, reason, and reflection to override our emotions. This is critical if we are able to form lasting, intimate relationships that benefit both partners. Without the ability to research, reason, and reflect we are creatures who use what were adaptive strategies in maladaptive ways.

Living a principled life is the only way that we can ascertain whether or not we are safe or threatened in an intimate relationship. However, it is extremely important that both people are capable of living a principled life to make a relationship work. If we chose to live a principled life and our partner does not, then we must always be suspect of what our partner is saying, thinking, or doing. In other words, our partner is susceptible to negotiating his or her values, beliefs, and principles based on the threat or safety sensed at any given moment in time. So what advantage is there to living a principled life if our partner does not opt to do this?

When we live a principled life, we are freer of the constraints placed on us by our emotions. We have more choices about what to do about any given situation. Our lives are more productive and goad directed. We can experience a full range of rich emotions and feelings without fearing that we will be harmed. We use our research, reason, and reflection to solve problems. We know when a situation demands immediate action and when thought is our best strategy to ensure safety. From this vantage point, we are not constantly riding a roller coaster. Living a principled life gives us the best opportunity we have to experience living fully without repetitive crisis dictating life responses. Our relationships are calmer and less volatile. We are more connected in meaningful ways. We manage our Selves differently, more responsibly.

We have choices about whether or not we begin and/or continue relationships. We are free to choose to be in a relationship, and we are free to choose to end a relationship. This does not mean that we are robotic in nature. We must remember it is when we manage our own sense of threat and define a solid sense of Self that we are finally able to have a truly intimate relationship. Each sensory perception is fully alive. We have had to shut nothing down for our emotional comfort. We are not engaged in limit setting or game playing to keep our Selves safe. Those people who relate to us find a safe haven in the relationship. When a person senses safety, it means that he or she is more apt to engage in thought. With two people researching, reasoning, and reflecting a relationship is more likely to thrive.

We must remember, however, that our families are critical centers of learning. The more intensely a person has learned to be wary and shut off from a need to protect him or her Self, the more difficult management of Self will be. We must still use our emotions as a form of protection. Not all relationships are safe for us, no matter how principled we are in our behavior. This is the importance of knowing the distinction between Self and another person. We can behave from a principled position and reject a relationship. It is possible. As we try to understand how the idea link to our lives, an example may help.

Leslie had gathered some information, she had come to identify and understand some patterns that operated in her family, and she could easily see that some of her family had behaved in a very Selfish or a very Selfless way. She could see how people in her family had engaged in emotional responses as ways to protect them Selves. In other words, Leslie had a fairly neutral view of what had happened in her family. Although she still saw people in her family as being responsible for how they managed them Selves, she found her Self being less critical of her family for the life decisions they had made. What Leslie also found was that she was less critical about her own life.

The mistakes that she had made up to this point in her life seemed like the natural outcome of having limited strategies available to her. She could see how the strategies she had used up to now were maladaptive for the solutions she desired. Leslie decided to go further and begin to explore issues related to her values, beliefs, and principles. Her therapist agreed to help her with this, and they arranged that Leslie would see him once a month. With some new skills to problem-solve, Leslie was comfortable with working at this pace. She spent the time between sessions working on defining her Self. She thought of her therapist as a coach to whom she could report her thoughts. He helped her to work on understanding patterns and managing her emotions. She worked on defining her values, beliefs, and principles, and her coach helped her to assess if her behaviors reflected her values, beliefs, and principles. Leslie knew that as she dealt with others if she saw that what a person said they valued and believed was not reflected in their behavior that they had defined a Self that was very attuned to the sense of threat they experienced. This was invaluable to Leslie, as she could determine how much she could depend on this person.

She found that her relationships with others slowed down. When she met someone, she listened to what they told her about themselves and watched to see if their behavior matched. She also listened to what she told others about herself and then monitored her own behavior. When she found her Self saying one thing and behaving in the opposite way, it gave her an indication that she was experiencing a threat to her Self or that the relationship was not forming the connection that she wanted. She had reliable gauges she could use to help her manage her emotions. When Leslie started working on defining her values, beliefs, and principles, she had an additional tool to help her to define her Self more solidly.

Leslie started by just listing her values, beliefs, and principles. She listed a value, and then she listed the belief beside the value. In other words, she tried to answer the question: what makes this value important to me? From there she listed the behavior she would expect from holding the value and the belief. Suddenly Leslie could see that each situation in her life was not some kind of puzzle. She could see that each situation had a solution if she used her values, beliefs, and principles as guides. The next step for Leslie was to determine which of her values, beliefs, and principles she had been living and which of those she had not been using. After Leslie had distinguished between these, she asked her Self the following questions: how did I decide that this was important to me? How do I know that this is an accurate conclusion to draw? What are the consequences if I behave this way?

Leslie began to see her Self from a whole different perspective. As Leslie began to answer the question how did I decide what was important to me, she looked to her family to see what she might have learned from them. She used the facts she had gathered and the patterns that she understood from her family. Leslie discovered that the sense of threat she experienced when she was not in a relationship had something to do with her parents having not had fathers in their lives as they grew up. Each had experienced threats to their well-being in many different ways, because they did not have fathers to help to raise them. Both of her parents thought that a father was very important to a family. Both her parents had stayed in a fairly unhappy marriage based on the belief that fathers add stability to a family and that women cannot function stably independent of a man. Her parents had made life decisions based on their values and beliefs. Leslie had learned from them.

As Leslie had grown up, she had taken sides about what went on between her mother and father. She had believed that her mother was the victim in the relationship, and that her mother did not protect her Self from her husband the way she should have. Leslie had grown up learning to value taking care of your Self instead of relying on a man to take care of you. She also valued having a man, because her parents had taught her that life without a man was indeed a threat. Suddenly, Leslie could see that her behaviors were based on what she had learned from her parents. She could see that she exhibited behaviors of desperation to secure a relationship, and she could see that any evidence that a man was treating her like her mother had been treated resulted in her dumping the relationship. The treats she experienced seemed reasonable although not logical given the facts.

Leslie saw that she was giving up her Self to secure the relationship and then demanding Self back from someone who was not aware of her emotions. Leslie saw her Self behaving much like her mother did. She also saw her father in a new light, and realized that the confusion he must experience contributed to his irresponsible decisions. Leslie now had some points of intervention. The added bonus was that Leslie no longer wondered if she had some kind of psychiatric disorder. She knew that she was like everyone else in experiencing two forces converging on her life. Another added bonus was that she became more neutral with her parents and calmer about their situation. As she did, she watched both her parents become more thoughtful and less conflicted with one another. Leslie had set out to work only on her Self, and she was seeing improvements all around her.

The area of improvement about which Leslie was most pleased was that she was gaining more certainty about who she was as a Self. Her work place became a different place for her. She did not want someone at work to take care of her anymore, so her relationships with her co-workers shifted dramatically. She became more involved in groups and activities that really mattered to her, and she found her Self being more creative. She enjoyed being with her family at a very different level, and instead of avoiding them, she started to see them more frequently. They seemed to enjoy her company as well. Her friends commented on how much more relaxed she seemed. And, she had started dating a man she met.

For the first time in her life, she was simply dating. She was aware that she was a distinct Self from this man and that there would be times that because of their individual differences that they would not be together. She realized that she would not die if the relationship ended, so she could relax and enjoy her activities when she was away from him. Leslie recognized that she and Ryan would not like the same people and should not expect to always have to be together when their friends were with them. She was a Self, and Ryan was a Self. She did not take on more responsibility for the relationship than she wanted to. In fact, Ryan did her laundry on occasion. Leslie sensed that she was in a partnership. As a result of being more of a Self, Leslie was less reactive in her relationship with Ryan. She was much more comfortable and not always on edge about everything little thing that happened. Ryan seemed comfortable as well. Leslie found her Self being dependable. When she expressed her needs or stated a position about something, her behavior was consistent.

The relationship with Ryan had its ups and downs, but the ups and downs were smaller than any Leslie had ever experienced. When she sensed that she was becoming reactive and was having difficulty engaging her thought, she made an appointment to see her therapist and got a little objectivity from him. She found the process helpful to her. She was also seeing her therapist less and less frequently now. As she was gaining experience at thinking, she found that she was learning how to become more objective without him. She was reminded of the Mona Lisa and the flashing traffic lights often as she worked her way through difficult situations. When a situation was particularly intense, she found her Self more apt to react in the ways that she had before. But, her reactions were less intense. Leslie decided that being a Self was a lifelong process, and she also decided the rewards were worth it. Fireflies must rely on certain adaptive strategies to work for them. Compared to the strategies we have, fireflies are limited in their responses. We must use the adaptive advantages that we have to reach our potential beyond that of a firefly. Our relationships are more complex: how we behave requires more complex strategies. These strategies are available to us. All we have to do is to use them, but we need to know what they are.

We must recognize that we are separate people and that the distinction is to our advantage. We must realize that we are highly reactive creatures prone to error and stop to think through our life situations. We must define a Self that is solid and welcome relationships as sources of support and strength. We can have both. We do not have to circulate through bars trying to get someone to care for us while we pretend to be someone we are not. We can be our Selves. This is all possible, because we can know what we need to know to make our relationships work.

END OF CHAPTER WORK

Review the chapter and as you do, think about what ideas were most important to you. How do you think that idea could be of some help to you?

List your own values, beliefs, and principles. How much do your behaviors reflect what you say you value and believe?

Review the list you just made (the process may take several days, weeks or months). Try to separate between the values and beliefs that seem to be helpful to you and those that are not helpful to you. It is important to understand the origin of these values and beliefs and to determine if these really are the values and beliefs you have. You will know if your behavior matches what you say you value and believe.

CHAPTER SIX

Knowing When to Call It Quits

Deep in dark oceans where no light penetrates the water angler fish mate. The connection that occurs with the mating of these two fish links them to one another in remarkable ways. The linkage provides these two fish their mechanism for reproducing. As with other forms of life, this mating takes its toll. Both the male fish and the female fish give up part of their individual identity to mate. These fish, however, give up their individual identities to the extreme.

The male angler fish, considered to be parasitic, bites the flesh of the female and attaches to the female anglerfish with what appears as a tube connecting the two fish together. The tube functions much the same way as an umbilical cord does between human mothers and their offspring. Just as the human umbilical cord pumps life giving nutrients to an unborn child, the male anglerfish receives total nourishment through this tube. The female's circulatory system becomes his circulatory system, and he is dependent on her to manage for both of them. The female, in essence, becomes responsible for his life. She in turn has her eggs fertilized for reproduction. Each gains something from the relationship, but each being gives up his/her individuality to a large degree. She must supply him life sustaining nutrients, and he loses his freedom to move about on his own.

Each fish has compromised individual functioning in service of mating. While one can still characterize the two fish as individuals, one must also see the interdependence that has developed between them. It becomes difficult to think of these fish as two individuals, and indeed, individual functioning has now become dependent on another being. Because of how they are linked to one another, the distinctions that we would typically think of as constituting an individual become blurred. The functioning of one fish becomes a factor in the well being of the other fish. If the functioning of one is diminished, the other fish experiences the impact. If one experiences stimuli in a specific way, the chemical reactions of that fish pulses through the body of the other fish. Individual responses blur as one reacts to the reaction of the first. They are linked to one another in complex ways that alters the experiences that one individual would have had alone. The other fish, thus adding a degree of complexity to understanding "individual" behavior, experiences what happens to its mate. The fish have compromised individual functioning to form a relationship that results in reproduction. How mutually beneficial such an attachment is depends on what price each individual pays to maintain the attachment. Obviously with angler fish, the female expends life energy to support two organisms instead of just herself. This type of compromise of individual functioning can be found among many species.

In our own species, we are encouraged to give up our individuality and function as one when we become intimate with another person. Expectations soar that the other person will behave in context with us carefully. It is our dream, our hope for a special connection that gives us a sense of completion and wholeness. We desire to be special, wanted, and accepted for who we are. As we push for that acceptance, the very expectation begins to push us to compromise who we are----a dilemma of major proportions. On the one hand we want to be loved for who we are, and yet, we are expected to function as one, a demand that means we must alter at least some of who we are. The contradiction does not occur to us. We move into a relationship without a clear picture of exactly what that means. As we have learned, both nature and nurture impact our functioning in relationships. We have discovered that we are prone to err in our perceptions of what happens to us in our relationships. It is important to distinguish what is a real threat from what is not. When we pause to think about both nature and nurture in our relationships, we can begin to make decisions about the relationship itself. Decisions that are build upon research, reason, and reflection given that we have defined our values, beliefs, and principles are usually decisions that are sound. If we are asking our Selves if our relationships are a little bit too much like the angler fish described above, then we need to assess whether or not to stay in the relationship.

NATURE

Nature arms us with adaptive strategies. These strategies are supposed to ensure our safety. The strategies that we have available to us depend on what perceptual system we are using with each situation we encounter. The first perceptual system that we use to assess all information is our *emotional system*. The emotional system is designed to sense threat or safety and to allow us an automatic response. In a crisis, we need to respond automatically. That may save our lives. What we need to be aware of when we are assessing whether or not we need to end a relationship is what degree of "real threat" we face.

In making such an assessment, we must recognize if a threat exists to our physical self. Any physical contact in which partners are striking one another is an indicator that physical separation is in our best interests. No matter how much one wants to dismiss the incident, it is important until one has researched the facts, understands the factors that contributed to the incident, and reflects on the safety of each person that physical separation occur. The relationship itself may be viable, but physical safety needs to be assured. If one spouse is opposed to the separation, that spouse is operating from a sense of threat. The threat needs to be addressed. Physical threat presents an obvious situation that the relationship may need to end, however, threats to our sense of Self are not as clear to assess.

If in a relationship, our partner suggests that our perceptions and interpretations are in error and we discover that indeed we are not in error and the facts were available to our partner, we need to assess for the degree of threat we face in the relationship. Questioning our perceptions and interpretations as being grounded in reality requires a great deal of life energy. The confusion that can result when we experience reality in one way only to be told by someone we love that our reality is distorted transfers the threat we perceive away from the relationship and directs it at our own functioning. We have to be concerned with our reality. A good example that occurs frequently happened with Jay and Glenda.

Jay and Glenda were in their second marriage. Glenda began to be concerned that Jay was having an affair with a woman at his work place. He was oftentimes late home from work, he smelled like perfume, and this woman was calling often to ask Jay to help her with things that seemed inappropriate to Glenda. Glenda asked her husband if he were involved with Jennifer. Jay denied any involvement. He told Glenda that she was being ridiculous and needed to work on trust issues. The situation got worse. Glenda was convinced that Jay was having an affair with Jennifer. Each time she approached him about the subject, he told her she needed to get some help. So, Glenda arranged for them to see a marriage therapist. Jay attended with Glenda faithfully.

Jay explained to the therapist that he had to work late with Jennifer, because they were on a team project. He told the therapist that Jennifer was single and knew no one in town and had called him on a few occasions for help. The therapist asked Glenda what evidence she had that Jay was having an affair. Glenda said it was an impression she had that was not built on any hard facts. She had not caught Jennifer and her husband together nor had anyone she knew seen them together. The therapist suggested that Glenda work on trust issues, and so Glenda started individual therapy. Each time she had an impression that Jay was involved with Jennifer she talked to herself about needing to trust her husband. She wanted to trust him. Soon Glenda was wondering about other perceptions she had and wondered if she were in error about those as well. More and more self-doubt crept into her daily experiences.

Glenda began to have trouble sleeping and was placed on medications for a depression. Her doctor suggested she come in more frequently for therapy sessions to help her deal with her self-esteem issues. Glenda felt like she was falling apart. Her marriage seemed to be in trouble, and yet, her husband denied that he thought it was in trouble.

In a few months, her husband came home from work and announced that he was being transferred at work to a new division. Glenda was very happy for him, but she was also relieved for herself. Now her husband would not have contact with Jennifer on a daily basis. Jennifer stopped calling their home, and Jay started spending more time with his family. Glenda began to feel better and stopped the anti-depressants. She was certain now that she had been imagining things and put extra effort into her marriage to make up to Jay for not trusting him. Jay seemed to really appreciate this and commented now and then that Jennifer needed to remember that she could trust him in the future.

He reminded her that he had to work with women sometimes on team projects. Within a few months, Jay was talking about Missy, a new woman on his team at work.

Glenda once again became suspicious of her husband. She sank back into a depression that this time was far deeper than the depression she had experienced before. She blamed herself for not being secure enough as a person to allow her husband to even do her job without her being accusatory. Eventually the doctor recommended a hospitalization to try to help her to alleviate the depression. Glenda was scheduled for electric shock therapy to help her get better again, when a friend of hers visited. The friend's husband had told her that Jay was having another affair at work. This friend was aware of the struggles Glenda was having and thought that she should know.

Glenda was enraged. She checked herself out of the hospital and went to an attorney's office. Glenda filed for a divorce. At the courtroom when the divorce was granted, Jay approached Glenda. He told her about all the affairs that he had been having over the years. He wanted her to know that she really was not crazy.

When we allow another person to tell us that our perceptions and interpretations are wrong, our self erodes. At times, we are in error, but at other times we are not. It is difficult to know for certain, but when our perceptions and interpretations differ greatly from our partners, and we are dismissed as crazy, it is important to determine if the relationship is in our best interest. No matter what the "truth" is, we are paying a dear price for the relationship. When we are in serious trouble based on what is happening between our partner and us, it is critical to determine if the relationship poses more threat to us than it is worth. Always, no matter what the situation, it is important for us to look at our Selves and understand what role we play in any given situation.

When we find our Selves not being our Selves in our intimate relationships, we must stop to assess the degree of threat that we face. We must determine how much this is a product of our own functioning and how much it is a product of our partner's functioning. Any work discriminating our Self from the other person will benefit us whether or not we continue in a relationship. Research, reason, and reflection will eventually help us to know what to do. If we react automatically and leave a relationship without research, reason, and reflection then our behavior may be based on a misperception or misinterpretation. Answering the question: Is this relationship in my best interest can give us a clue about what we need to do. Another set of questions needs to be answered to help us to know whether or not to end a relationship.

NURTURE

We learn from our families how to use adaptive strategies, and we define the degree of solid Self we have based on what we have learned. We do that through establishing values, beliefs, and principles. Anytime we have a situation in which we do not know what to do, if we focus on our values, beliefs, and principles, we will know the direction that would be most beneficial to us. Values, beliefs, and principles that have been based on research, reason, and reflection take into account the other people involved in the relationship system. In other words, well-defined values, beliefs, and principles are neither Selfish nor Selfless. Once we have defined our values, beliefs, and principles based on research, reason, and reflection, we can use these as tools to guide us through life's toughest decisions. If we are Selfish or Selfless, then we need to think about our values, beliefs, and principles again. Attempting to be aware of any sense of threat in decision-making will help us to know how clearly we have thought through our values, beliefs, and principles.

If we sense a need to protect our Selves by not considering the other people in the relationship system, then we are probably engaged in an emotional reaction. If we sense desperation to keep the relationship in tact, then we are probably engaged in an emotional reaction. A Self focused decision is relatively dispassionate. Our feelings are not pushing us around. We have made choices based on what is in the best interest of our Selves as well as others who are involved.

An extremely important marker that a relationship may not be viable is to determine how far apart our values, beliefs, and principles are from our partner. If extreme differences exist, it is important to assess the relationship for how much life energy will be required to continue the relationship. At times, the bottom line is that the relationship demands excessive amounts of life energy to keep it afloat. If it does, then it is a threat to our Self. It is important if we end a relationship based on extreme differences in values, beliefs, and principles to be clear about what attracted us to the relationship initially. Most likely we will find that we experience a high degree of threat when we think about being alone. We may be uncertain of how to take care of our Selves on our own. We can work through those issues and give our Selves choice. It is hard work, but it can be done.

The sense of threat may surface as we make tough decisions, but when the decisions are based on research, reason, and reflection, we will see our way through the challenge that we face. Ending a relationship cannot kill us. It may seem as if it can, but the facts are that it cannot. The facts that will help us are:

How distinct are we as a Self versus our partner? Have we blurred boundaries or allowed boundaries to be blurred to the point that we find it difficult to distinguish who we are? Do we sense threat when we think about being alone? Do we sense threat when we think about continuing the relationship?

Have we spent time researching, reasoning and reflecting to the point that we have gathered objective facts, understood how the facts fit together, and determined a course of action that considers the best interests of all concerned?

Have we defined our values, beliefs, and principles? Are our values, beliefs, and principles in extreme contrast to those of our partner?

As we look at a situation in which a man struggled with ending his relationship, we can see how some of these ideas apply to every day life.

Dena has been married to Robert for about five years. Their relationship has been extremely conflicted. When we look at the facts about the relationship we find that Dena has many complaints about Robert getting his way in the relationship. Both Robert and Dena decide to write down the major events in their marriage and to determine whose want and or need was the determining factor in the decision that was made. Once and for all, they were going to put this issue behind them.

Dena believed that Robert always made the decisions about their lives. She watched Robert as he was active in a few select groups and clubs: he had some interests that he pursued but also tried to support Dena with any interest she had. They sat down to make their lists.

When the list was completed, both Dena and Robert agreed that Dena made most of the major decisions they had made in the last five years. Dena apologized to Robert for accusing him of always having to have his way. The next major decision came along, and Robert was working to be more aware of his behavior. What he noticed was that he said what was important to him, Dena said she wanted the opposite. Robert went along with Dena to help her to see that he really did care about her being an equal partner. Soon Dena accused Robert of having made the decision. Robert reviewed the situation with Dean detailing the facts of the situation. Dena apologized again. The situation occurred over and over again.

It was important to Robert to get along in the relationship with Dena, but what was happening was that he was giving in more and more until he barely had any say in the relationship decisions at all. And, in addition to that, Dena never recognized that she was the one making the decisions. Robert valued getting along. He believed that if he showed his wife that he was flexible and cared about her having some say in the relationship that she would see that she was getting her way. Then they would get along with each other and be happy in their marriage. He gave in often to what she wanted. Her accusations became relentless. Robert did not know what to do.

The conflict escalated to the point that Robert decided to leave the relationship. He divorced Dena, and Dena was still accusing him of having everything his way. No matter how many facts Robert gave Dena to support that she was the person making the decision, within a short period of time, Dena was accusing him again. Once Robert was out of the relationship, he became aware that Dena had a point.

What Robert realized was that Dena always did the opposite of what he said he wanted. That meant that Robert was actually in charge of what happened in the relationship. Dena valued having an opinion. She believed that having an opinion of her own meant that she said the opposite of another person. So when someone said something, she simply said she wanted the opposite. Of course, it meant that Dena never got what she actually wanted, and the other person was indeed in charge.

When Robert looked at Dena's family to help him understand what prompted Dena to do this, he could easily see that Dena had never been allowed to have an opinion. Dena's family disregarded their children's wants or needs. When Dena told her mother she wanted something, her mother always told her that she did not really want that but wanted something else instead. Dena had never had what she wanted. Getting what she wanted became of extreme importance to her. The other thing that happened between Dena' mother and her was that Dena had always had to go along with her mother. Agreement meant that Dena had not gotten her way. So, Dena believed that to agree meant that she would not get her way. So, Dena's behavior made logical sense when we could see what had happened with her family. Dena was doomed to be in a conflicted relationship. It was the only way she could experience that she was a Self. Her values, beliefs, and principles were based on the sense of threat she experienced as she tried to be a Self. If Robert were going to be in this relationship, he would be constantly engaged in conflict in addition to compromising himself. Robert decided not to live his life that way.

Leaving a relationship is always a challenge. Leaving a relationship responsibly is a major challenge. Clearly defining Self, becoming more objective about the other person void of blame, and making decisions based on the good of each person in the systems requires a high degree of emotional maturity. At times, this is the wisest choice available in a relationship. Far too often, leaving a relationship is seen as a failure versus being the responsible thing to do. Guilt, being fearful of being seen as a failure, not wanting to live through the conflict of a divorce are poor excuses to stay in a relationship. Fear of leaving and being on one's own is a realistic fear. To do so, we must face what our fears are and become more realistic about whether or not these fears are well founded. Divorce alters the quality of life for everyone involved, in some way. It can also alleviate a great deal of tension, relieve symptoms that have become fixed in one or more persons, and give us a real opportunity to come to know our Selves better and learn skills that are more adaptive and functional. Making a relationship work is at minimum a two-person project. One person may decide to leave when another does not want to end the relationship.

Because one person ends a relationship with us does not mean that something is wrong with us. It may mean that something is very right with us. The situation presents a wonderful opportunity for Self-assessment. Changing who we are or promising to change who we are in attempts to convince a person to stay with us is a one way street to nowhere. Being who we really are, the positives as well as the negatives, presents the best chance we will ever have to find a relationship in which acceptance and love for who we are is possible. Pretending is never a helpful solution.

This book is about hope. This chapter represents another slant on hope. We sometimes need to quit. Quitting when a situation is damaging to one or more persons represents good common sense, not failure. Quitting gives us the opportunity of moving forward with our lives, thus giving us the opportunity to find a meaningful relationship in which both persons can find that for which they are seeking. It gives us the opportunity to help our children to sense relief in families where conflict is habitual or in which children are symptomatic. Quitting can help us to regain the life energy we need to re-assess our own lives, make changes, and move forward. We have options. We can live without a partner in our lives and deal with being on our own in constructive ways.

In many ways we are like angler fish. But we are not tied to one another for our very survival. We can be individuals, and we can be in relationships with others without paying such a high price. We do not have to be attached by umbilical cords. We can be attached by being strong Selves capable of thought, reason, and reflection. And when this is not possible with one particular person or it is not possible due to our own emotional immaturity, we can quit and go back to the drawing board. We do not have to be parasitic or give our Selves up to be preyed upon by parasites. We can use simple ideas that can help us to know what we need to know to make our relationships work.

END OF CHAPTER WORK

Answer the question: have both you and your partner focused life energy on defining a self in the context of the relationship? If you have and you still experience serious symptoms, then consider seriously the possibility of leaving the relationship.

List all the symptoms you see either in your self, your partner, and/or your children. Do you see these Symptoms as something you can resolve? It is important to get professional help with someone Who understands Bowen Family Systems Theory to help you assess what to do.

CHAPTER SEVEN

We Are Always Home

Far above our planet, removed from our atmosphere, we orbit our home. We construct a home away from home— a space station from which we may begin colonization beyond our own planet. Our species cannot exist in outer space without creating an environment in which we can adapt: an environment that is not hostile to our needs. We dedicate our selves to venture beyond what we know, but as we do so, we make this place of exploration as much like home as we possibly can. We move beyond necessity to create the conditions of our original home. We use laws, principles of science, to turn something foreign to us into something more familiar. Knowledge, gained from seeking the facts, permits us to explore the unfamiliar to us while we work to create circumstances that we know. Familiarity seems to help us adapt more quickly to the unknown. Our fears are lessened. We are calmer creatures. We do not sense our home as being so alien to us. We are not forced to learn as we go, to create solutions to problems as they arise: we have thought, we have reasoned, we have reflected. >From our thought, our reason, and our reflection, we have used our previous learning to help us predict our challenges. With accurate predictions, we plan strategies to manage the challenges we will face. In the midst of a challenge, we respond with methodical strategy: the outcome of forethought.

To make our new home more familiar, the space station we construct turns slowly as does our home planet. The rotation of our space station creates a centrifugal force that literally pushes us into the walls of the space station, giving the inhabitants, beings of our own kind, the sense of gravity. Even though the gravity we create is a "mock" gravity, we experience being anchored, much as we do to our own earth. Our movement is not confined to one specific place on the wall of the space station. We calculate the amount of centrifugal force needed to allow us the sensation of gravity as well as the freedom of movement.

With thought, we can anticipate that being pressed into a wall from which we cannot move does create a gravitational force like our planet has but would render us helpless to complete daily chores for our survival and advancement.

We can move about much as we do on our own planet. We experience forces similar to what we are accustomed when our feet are on planet earth, and yet, the force is different. We easily blur such differences with the result being that we are not aware of the differences. Our brains operate in such a way that does not require exact and precise replication of a sensation: we must come just close enough. As we approximate similarity, our brains simply fill-in the rest to create the "known". We can delude our selves quite easily.

We create in our relationships that which is familiar to us. We replicate patterns that we have learned in our families over and over again. We learned these patterns, but we select our behavior as human beings based on what nature has given us. It is the two forces, nature and nurture, that determines our intimate behavior. Both nature and nurture has given us options, but unless we know that we have options and need to use them, we are stuck in repetitive patterns of behavior that are resulting in intimate relationships providing little of what we are looking for.

Nature has provided us with adaptive strategies: all the adaptive strategies that we need. Our strategies range from pure emotions, to feelings, all the way to thought. The strategies are in place to help us in specific circumstances. Our emotions are designed to give us automatic reactions in dangerous situations. Our feelings are designed to help us to ascertain the degree of threat that we face based on our emotions. Our thoughts are designed to help us to research, reason, and reflect in more complex situations that may require a novel solution. We can depend on learning to help us to negotiate dangerous situations. We learn cues that represent danger and cues that represent safety. When we are not in a dangerous situation, then being able to problem-solve, gives us access to many behaviors. Complexity demands many different behaviors available to us.

When we sense threat, we have four choices: to run, to fight, to camouflage, or to play dead. None of these choices are really helpful to a relationship. We have the capacity to behave differently, but unless we can override the sense of threat to access our thought, we are simply stuck. When we react to our partner as if we need to protect our Selves from them, then it is highly likely that our partner will react to us. Since we always assess every situation in our lives for threat, then we must be aware that relationships require that more than that. When we are not a solid and distinct Self, we are more apt to sense threat in our relationships with our partners.

Nature has also armed us with feelings: the Subjective perceptual system. Our feelings are meant to help us to know the degree of threat we are actually facing. Our feelings help us to form connections and maintain them. Unfortunately we are prone to error in our assessments, and depending on our feelings to make life choices can result in making a life-decision that is a mistake for our well-being. Feelings can well up with intensity and then go flat. We may have made a major life decision when our feelings are heightened only to realize the decision was a mistake when our feelings subside. So, nature gave us yet another adaptive strategy to help us to deal with complex situations.

Our Objective perceptual system gives us the ability to research, reason, and reflect. This is the process of thought and gives us the greatest range of behaviors from which to choose. We can gather information, understand how the information fits together to determine our behavior, and then reflect on our Selves and others in a way that balances the need for self and other. When we are balanced in our need for a Self and our need for a relationship, we are not Selfish and not Selfless. This offers the opportunity for genuine intimacy, openness, and a meaningful connection with a rich range of emotions and feelings.

We must remember that we are separate and distinct Selves, that we always assess for threat, and that we need to be a Self and we need to have a relationship. These are the basic ways that we behave in our intimate relationships. Our nature and nurtures interact to determine the behavior we will express in reference to these basic factors. Nature is inherent in that we come equipped. Nurture is what we learn.

We learn from our families whether or not a stimulus in our environment should be interpreted as a threat or as safe. We learn this very early in life, so that by the time we enter school, patterns of behavior are pretty much set in place. This begins at birth, and we learn whether or not we experience relationships as threatening or safe. Depending on if our families see the world as a safe place for us to explore and develop we will either flourish or restrict our Selves. If we are free to explore, we can learn skills important to our becoming an independent human being who is a solid Self. This will determine how much we react to our relationships versus being able to think.

When we are able to think, we can define a solid sense of Self. We do this by defining our values, beliefs, and principles. We determine what is important to us, we determine what we is accurate, and we determine how to behave based on what is important and what is accurate. When we behave based on values, beliefs and principles that are the product of research, reason, and reflection, we have access to rich relationships and a solid sense of Self. This is the formula to sense safety. From safety, we can become our very best Selves. This is based on a different way of thinking, a different way of understanding our Selves.

Bowen Family Systems Theory gives to us the first way to see our Selves as simply human beings who are using adaptive strategies in maladaptive ways. The theory describes how nature and nurture impacts who we are and how we behave in our intimate relationships with one another. The theory unlocks relationship mysteries that have dumbfounded us and have taken us to divorce courts in droves. It allows us the possibility to come close to one another, to define strong senses of Self, and to experience our Selves and our relationships totally. We do not have to cut-off from any aspect of our Selves, and we do not have to cut-off from each other. The most important thing that Bowen Family Systems Theory offers us is tools: effective tools. These tools can allow us to work through relationship challenges and give our relationships a chance. There is hope: we have all the adaptive strategies we need to make our relationships work. And, now, we have what we need to know.

Printed in the United States
16399LVS00001B/538-636